JOURNEY TO THE JACKSONS

♪

A Mother's Bold & Extraordinary Actions to make her Child's Seemingly Impossible Dream Come True

BY

SLOAN J. LUCKIE

"Only those who dare to fail greatly, can ever achieve greatly"
—Robert Kennedy

In Loving Memory of My Mother
Sodonia R. Luckie
(1922–1992)

CONTENTS

PREFACE

It was June 25th, 2009. A beautiful day in Chicago. The clear blue sky was only outdone by the radiant sun that seemed to sit above it. My wife, Sherree, and I were with our two youngest children, Sloan, seven years old and Sterling, five years old. We were traveling back home to the south suburbs of Chicago after spending a beautiful sunny day at the Brookfield Zoo. After entering a ramp with a nearby sign that read "I-94E to I-57S," I'd received a call on my cell phone. As I glanced at the caller ID, I noticed it was my sister Colette calling. She had moved to San Francisco after living in Chicago for approximately ten years. Colette would often call to brag about how beautiful the weather was in the Golden State. For this call, I was prepared to share the details of the beautiful weather we were having in "Chitown."

I answered the phone to hear Colette crying. "Michael passed away today."

"What did you say?" I asked incredulously. Though I heard her, I found it difficult to believe what I was hearing. I never questioned which Michael she was referring to.

"Michael is gone…" she responded, followed by complete silence.

"Michael has died?" I said aloud. Sherree, who was sitting in the passenger seat next to me, stared at me in total shock. Her phone began to ring. A relative of hers was calling to share the same sad news I had received from Colette. Sherree then called several friends and family members to confirm the report. Some said they'd heard he'd been rushed to the hospital and was in critical condition. Others claimed that he had passed. Still in disbelief, I turned on my radio to hear the same news of Michael Jackson's untimely and unfortunate death.

"Michael Jackson died?" my older son, Sloan, asked. Unaware that our children were listening intently to the breaking news on the radio, I answered him, "Yes, buddy, I believe he has."

Both Sloan and Sterling were saddened by the news. They'd recently watched a DVD we had of Michael performing "Billy Jean" on the Motown 25 television special. Even at young ages, they were completely mesmerized by Michael's dancing ability. After answering my son, I returned to my phone call with Colette. "Colette, are you there?"

"Yes," Colette answered with a voice that seemed to crack. We spent the rest of the time consoling each other. It was as if a family member had passed.

Days after Michael's passing, I had a casual phone conversation with my close friend, Jim Reynolds, the founder of Loop Capital. "Terrible about Mike. He was truly gifted," Jim said.

"Yes. It's really sad. It's as if a family member died," I responded.

"Wait! Didn't you tell me a story years ago, when we worked at Merrill Lynch, of how you spent a couple days with Michael and the Jackson family back in the seventies?" Jim asked.

"Yes, my sister, Colette, was his biggest fan. My mother, who had little money at the time, wanted Colette to live her dream of meeting Michael Jackson."

"That's right, I remember now." Jim began to recall the story. "Didn't you guys go to California by bus?"

"Yes," I said. "My mother used food stamps, welfare checks, and any other money she could borrow to pay for Greyhound bus tickets from New York's Port Authority to Los Angeles, California. We didn't even know where Michael Jackson and his family lived. It's amazing what mothers will do for their children."

"So true," Jim responded. I continued to tell the story, and Jim listened intently, recalling the story I had told him many years before.

Suddenly Jim spoke. "Sloan, I hate to interrupt you, but I'd like to make calls to a few TV news anchors I know here in Chicago. I think they'd find your story inspirational. I'll call you back in an hour."

Thirty minutes later, Jim called back. "Sloan, I just spoke with several anchors. I don't know who will call you, but they all appeared to be interested in your story. You should hear from at least one of them within a day or two."

An hour later, I got another call. "Hello, Sloan. This is Marion Brooks, with NBC News Chicago. Jim shared your story of how you, your sister, and your mother spent two days with Michael Jackson and the Jackson family. I'd love for you to come to the studio so I can interview you. I believe many people would be inspired by your story."

The following day, my wife and I arrived at the studio. A smiling Marion Brooks greeted us in the lobby of the NBC Universal building east of Michigan Avenue, also known as the "Magnificent Mile."

"Hello, I'm Marion." She shook my hand, and I introduced my wife.

Marion escorted us through the studio. We passed by waist-high cubicles where reporters sat, feverishly working on the next big story. In the distance, I noticed bright lights hanging from the ceiling pointed toward the large mahogany table where the anchor and co-anchor sat to deliver Chicago's latest news. Marion led us to a small newsroom. The newsroom contained a couple of tall lights that seemed to shine as bright as the sun. In the left corner of the room a TV camera stood on a large tripod. With Sherree waiting outside the room, Marion introduced me to her cameraman and directed me to a seat opposite her own. "Sloan, you'll sit over there." As I sat in the chair, the cameraman hooked a small microphone to the collar of my shirt.

Behind my chair was a PC screen that contained a still image of Michael Jackson. He wore a black sequined jacket with his world-famous glittering white glove that matched a dazzling white armband. The rest of the world and I became familiar with this outfit, which he wore for his memorable performance of "Billy Jean" on Motown's twenty-fifth anniversary TV broadcast and during live concert performances before hundreds of thousands of adoring fans.

The cameraman cued Marion. "So, Sloan, tell us how you met Michael Jackson and the Jackson family." With studio lights shining and camera rolling, I began to tell the story. "Well, Marion, it was the summer of 1973, a year I'll never forget…"

SODONIA

My mother, Sodonia Luckie, arrived in New York City with her three children Cecil Jr., Robert, and L'Tanya in 1954. Years before, they'd lived on March Field Air Force Base in Riverside, California with her husband Cecil, an air force sergeant. In 1950, Sodonia's husband was assigned to a base in French Morocco where she and her children would live for several years. After moving there, Sodonia's husband became increasingly abusive to her and developed a reputation as a womanizer. Sodonia made many attempts to flee. In the summer of 1954, Sodonia planned her final attempt at escaping. She had become more familiar with his schedule and decided to wait late in the evening. He'd begun getting late-night assignments on the base and would spend the remainder of the evening womanizing on the streets of Casablanca. On the night of her planned escape she had Cecil Jr., Robert, and L'Tanya get fully dressed as if they were going out.

"You want us to wear our outside clothes to bed, Ma?" Cecil Jr. asked.

"Yes, Cecil. I want you, Robert, and L'Tanya to put on your clothes tonight and get under the covers," she whispered. All three children lay under the covers fully dressed, with shoes on their feet. Sodonia wore her clothes under a nightgown she'd often wear to bed.

Her husband left the house at midnight. Shortly after he departed, she got her children out of bed. She grabbed the Samsonite suitcase, which she had packed the night before, from under their bed. She and her children met with a senior officer. "My husband has been abusive to me. Me and my children are leaving!"

"Where are you going to go, Mrs. Luckie?" the officer asked.

"Back to the States. New York City. We have to get the first plane out of here!"

Noticing Sodonia's sense of urgency, the officer said, "Well, the only plane that is leaving tonight is a paratrooper plane. It leaves in about an hour."

"We'll take that!" Sodonia replied.

An hour later, the officer put Sodonia and her children in a jeep and drove them to the tarmac to board the huge paratrooper plane. The plane had a row of bucket seats that rested against the wall of the plane. Unlike a commercial plane, the seats were lined up on each side of the plane facing each other. A paratrooper who accompanied them fastened Sodonia into her seat with a series of seat belts that crossed the front of her body. He then did the same for Cecil Jr., Robert, and L'Tanya. The children were so small that their feet dangled from the edges of the seats. Sodonia left French Morocco and her husband. She planned to start a new life in New York City.

● ● ●

The pace of the Big Apple surprised Sodonia, who was originally from Junction City, Kansas. Everyone seemed to do everything fast. Walk. Talk. Eat. New Yorkers did everything as if there were no tomorrow. With all her belongings in one case, $300 concealed in her bra, and three small children in tow, Sodonia headed to Harlem, an area of New York she'd only read about.

She checked into a hotel just east of 125th Street. "How much does it cost to stay here for a night?" Sodonia asked the short balding hotel owner.

"How much you got, pretty lady?"

"Three hundred dollars," she said innocently.

"That will do," the hotel owner replied.

From Sodonia's response and non-New York City accent, the grungy hotel owner sensed she wasn't from the area. She was a sheep among wolves. He took her $300 and gave her keys to the room.

The room was old and smelled of cigarette smoke. There were cracks in the walls and ceiling. The room was dim. Its only source of light was a 40-watt bulb in a socket in the middle of the ceiling. The bathroom was filthy. The tub had a rust ring and appeared as if it hadn't been cleaned since World War I. The mattress where they were to sleep had holes and no bed covers.

"Sleep with your clothes on," Sodonia told her children as they prepared for bed. She turned off the low-wattage light in the already dim room. All three children slept together in the small bed, and Sodonia slept in a nearby chair. As she sat in the chair, she could hear the bathroom sink dripping. She also seemed to hear what sounded like tiny feet running across the wood floor. Suddenly, she heard Cecil Jr., Robert, and L'Tanya begin to cry. When she turned on the light, there were water bugs crawling on the floor and in the bed where the children lay. L'Tanya screamed immediately. Sodonia chased the water bugs that were near her children. Cecil Jr. and Robert jumped up and whisked away the inch-long water bugs and assisted their younger sister in doing the same. The multilegged nocturnal critters then scattered back toward the walls like thieves in the night. Sodonia and her children slept with the light on. Their first night in New York City was a miserable one.

The next morning, Sodonia took her children and headed to the front desk. "There were water bugs everywhere! We could hardly sleep last night. I want my money back!" Sodonia exclaimed.

"Well, that's not going to happen, country girl. If you don't like it, you can get out of here!"

Sodonia left the hotel in tears with her suitcase, Cecil Jr., Robert, and L'Tanya walking behind her like ducklings following their mother. Sodonia sat on top of her suitcase with L'Tanya in her lap, and Cecil Jr. and Robert sat on the concrete sidewalk with their feet dangling off the sidewalk curb. Overwhelmed by her plight, Sodonia began to cry. She had no money, she was new to New York City, her kids were hungry, and they had no place to stay. A woman who noticed Sodonia asked, "What's wrong, honey? Can I help?"

With tears streaming down her face, Sodonia began to explain. "I gave the owner of this hotel three hundred dollars to rent a room. It's all I had. The room was filthy. Whenever I turned the lights off to go to bed, large water bugs would come out of the walls. They were crawling on my children. When I complained and demanded my money back, he kicked us out."

The woman was livid. "Don't you worry. I'll get your money back!" The woman marched toward the hotel with her purse dangling from her left arm. Resembling Tyler Perry's character, Madea, the woman stood over six feet tall and weighed approximately three hundred pounds. She pushed open the hotel doors with such force that they made a loud crashing sound as each struck a nearby wall. The hotel manager's eyes were wide with fear as the big-boned woman approached him.

"Look'a here, little man!" The woman started her tirade as she stood over the short man with her finger in his face. "You see that woman out there?" She pointed at Sodonia, sitting on her suitcase. "She gave you three hundred dollars to stay in this rat hole! If you don't give that money back, I'm gonna wrap this purse handle around your little neck and only let go after you stop breathing!"

Without uttering a word, the hotel manager immediately reached into his cash register and handed $300 to the woman. The woman snatched the money out of the man's hand. As she approached the door, she kicked the doors, causing a crash as loud as when she had entered. She walked out the hotel and calmly said to Sodonia, "Here's your money, honey."

"Thank you so much, Ms...."

"Ms. Joyce, honey. My name is Ms. Joyce. What is your name?"

"Sodonia. Sodonia Luckie."

"Do you and your children have a place to stay, Sodonia?" Ms. Joyce asked.

"No, we don't. We just arrived in New York City yesterday." Sodonia told her that she had left her abusive husband and wanted to start a new life in New York City.

Ms. Joyce took Sodonia and her children to the local Red Cross center for food and clothing. The Red Cross volunteers provided them with milk and peanut butter and jelly sandwiches. A supervisor suggested that Ms. Joyce take Sodonia and her children to the local welfare office to receive financial assistance. "Do you have a place to stay?" the Red Cross supervisor asked.

"No, ma'am," Sodonia said.

"She can rent one of my rooms," Ms. Joyce interjected. "Since you don't have a place to stay, you can rent one of my rooms. It's clean."

Ms. Joyce had a large apartment in the Bronx to accommodate her common-law husband, Franklin Carter, and their seven children. Ms. Joyce took Sodonia to the public assistance office to receive aid for her and her children. After Sodonia completed mountains of paperwork, she looked at Ms. Joyce with eyes that were filled with tears of joy.

Ms. Joyce, fully understanding Sodonia's expression, said, "Let's go home."

Those words were like a sweet melody to Sodonia's ears. Sodonia wiped the tears from her eyes. She picked up her suitcase, and she and her children followed Ms. Joyce out of the public assistance office. They arrived at Ms. Joyce's apartment on Minford Place, just off Boston Road near Crotona Park, in the Bronx, New York.

Ms. Joyce brought Sodonia and her children into the living room to meet Mr. Carter. He was a tall, well-built man with a Native American complexion and hazel-colored eyes. "Carter, this is Sodonia Luckie and her children Cecil Jr., Robert, and L'Tanya. She's going to be renting a room from us."

"Hello, Sodonia. Nice to meet you and your children," a congenial Mr. Carter said with a Cheshire cat smile that displayed his ivory-white teeth.

Ms. Joyce's apartment had a long corridor that had rooms on each side. There were seven rooms in all. Three on one side of the corridor and four on the other. Each room had French doors at its entrance. Sodonia and her kids were given a room at the end of the corridor. The room had a bed, a small card table, and a rocking chair. Though the room was small, it was well lit and a lot cleaner than the roach-infested hotel room in Harlem. Cecil Jr., Robert, and L'Tanya would sleep in the bed, and Sodonia was to sleep in the rocking chair. After their nightmarish first twenty-four hours in New York, they'd finally get a goodnight's sleep. Sodonia lived in Ms. Joyce's apartment from 1954 to 1957. During this time, she finalized her divorce from her husband, Cecil. Ms. Joyce would become one of Sodonia's dearest friends.

● ● ●

One evening, Sodonia, Ms. Joyce, Mr. Carter, and the ten children between them were eating dinner together. Mr. Carter had an idea. "Hey, Sodonia, I got a buddy of mine I want you to meet. He's a real nice guy. Kinda quiet. Hard worker. His name is Sloan. Sloan Harris. I'm going to bring him by here this weekend."

"That's a good idea, Carter. Sodonia, you may like him. He's a real nice guy," Ms. Joyce said. My mother agreed to meet Sloan. Once Mr. Carter left the room, Ms. Joyce whispered, "And he's handsome, too," followed by a wink.

Sloan Harris and Mr. Carter were best friends. They both worked for a private New York City sanitation company. One day after work, Mr. Carter was talking to Sloan. "Hey, man, you have to meet this real pretty lady Joyce has staying in one of our rooms. She is gorgeous. A real looker. Her name is Sodonia."

"Sodonia?" Sloan asked. "What kind of name is that?"

"I think she's Mexican or Puerto Rican. But none of that will matter, man, once you see her," Mr. Carter retorted, followed by his Cheshire cat grin.

The following Saturday, Sloan met Sodonia. Mr. Carter called my mother out of the back room. "Hey, Sodonia, can you come out here? I want you to meet someone."

Sodonia came through the French doors that served as entryway to the room where she and the kids were staying. She had jet-black wavy hair that came down her shoulders. Her bronze complexion was accentuated by her ruby-red lipstick. She wore a blue Jane Russell-style dress that complemented her curves.

"Sloan, this is Sodonia," Mr. Carter introduced them. With his baritone voice, Sloan responded, "Hello, Sodonia, nice to meet you." He reached out to shake her hand. Sloan was a handsome, dark-skinned, muscular man. He was immediately attracted to her. Sloan thought she was not only beautiful but also congenial. Ironically, Sloan was taciturn and conservative. Apparently, opposites attract.

Sodonia and Sloan began to date. Sloan cared for Cecil Jr., Robert, and L'Tanya as if they were his own. He would take them to Crotona Park to play on the jungle gym. He attended their birthday parties, bearing gifts. Cecil Jr., Robert, and L'Tanya liked Sloan. They grew as emotionally attached to him as he had to them and their mother.

During the summer of 1957, Sodonia moved from Minford Place to 738 Metcalf Avenue, in the Clason Point housing project in the South Bronx. Clason Point, the grounds of a military academy between 1883 and 1927,[1] consisted of barrack-like apartments occupied by low-income residents. The apartments were around seven hundred square feet and separated by paper-thin walls. The walls were so thin that Sodonia and her children could clearly hear what their neighbors were saying and doing. Periodically, the children would place their ears against the walls

---

1   "Clason Point, Bronx," http://en.wikipedia.org/wiki/
    Clason_Point,_Bronx (October 13, 2013).

for better reception. They could hear couples arguing, gossiping, and making love.

Sodonia discovered Robert pressing his ear against the bedroom wall. "Ma, why is the woman next door moaning and the man making all kinds of strange noises?" Robert innocently asked. Having no interest in explaining sex, Sodonia said, "Robert, just get your ear away from that wall and stay out of grown folks' business!" Cecil Jr., Robert, and L'Tanya loved the neighborhood. There was a large play area out front. Across the street, a huge grassy area, known as the big field, was home to pheasants and rabbits. They easily grew accustomed to their new surroundings, as the apartments resembled the March Field Air Force barracks in Riverside, California, where they'd been based for several years.

• • •

Sodonia and Sloan continued to date. On January 6, 1960, they had their first child, Colette. On June 15, 1965, I was born. Like most African American kids in my neighborhood, my mother gave me a nickname that did not resemble my given name, Sloan. The nickname was Googie. She tried other nicknames like Frankie, Butchie, and others before coming to her final decision. Apparently I never responded to any of them. Then one day while I was in the crib, she looked at me and said, "Googie." I looked up at her and smiled. Googie was the nickname of a local football hero from Junction City, Kansas.

After I was born, Sloan offered to marry Sodonia. Sodonia, however, refused his proposal. Though she loved Sloan, she wasn't in love with him. Some of Sodonia's friends, who were also single parents, thought she was crazy for turning down such a proposal. "You can learn to be in love with him," some would claim. Sodonia, however, would not capitulate to peer pressure. Her decision to turn down his proposal took a considerable amount of courage. Many single mothers would not turn down an opportunity to have a stable provider. In spite of the economic hardship of raising two children on her own, she decided that she'd only marry for love. About a year after I was born, my mother and father stopped dating. As we grew older, Colette and I had weekly visits with our father, who had moved to Grand Concourse Village, located a few blocks away from Yankee Stadium in the Bronx.

Colette and I were raised in the same Clason Point apartment as our older brothers and sister who'd lived there before moving into their own apartments in the Bronx. The neighborhood in which we grew up was ethnically mixed. Clason Point predominantly comprised "Afro-Americans" (as we were called during the seventies) and "Nuyoricans" (New Yorkers of Puerto Rican descent). Unlike neighboring projects such as Soundview, Bronx River, Bronxdale, and others that consisted of buildings approximately ten stories high, our seven-hundred-square-foot Clason Point apartment had only two levels.

The first level included a ten by fourteen living room. Against one wall was a medium-size forest-green patterned couch wrapped with a clear hard-plastic covering. Opposite the couch sat an old secondhand floor model television. Emerging from behind the TV were two wire hangers wrapped in aluminum foil that replaced the rabbit-ear antennas needed for reception. Over time, the TV dial became inoperable, requiring us to use pliers to change the channel.

Along another wall rested an old secondhand piano that was given to my mother. Some of the once-white piano keys were chipped and had browned with age. Several other keys were inoperable, making a thudding sound instead of the melodious note intended. The living room also contained a small closet with a dull weathered-wooden door that looked as if it were a hundred years old. In the closet hung our "snorkels," paper-thin winter coats with a shiny outer layer and doglike fur around the hood. We'd also keep some of our favorite toys and board games in the small living room closet. Our favorites included Rock 'em Sock 'em Robots, Magic 8-Ball, Etch-A-Sketch, a Slinky, Monopoly, Mouse Trap, and a few other popular toys and board games of the early seventies.

Beyond the living room was our small kitchen. Our kitchen was approximately ten by ten feet. It contained a kitchen table that needed a book under one leg to keep plates from sliding off. We had an old white refrigerator with a matching stove, both of which seemed like they were from World War I.

On the second level were a small bathroom and two small bedrooms, all of which had old doors like the closet in the living room. As with the windows downstairs, all the windows upstairs had grates to keep out marauders. The bathroom had a volatile plumbing system. If someone flushed the toilet while the other was in the shower, it caused scolding hot water to spew from the showerhead.

Colette slept in the smaller bedroom, which was eight by thirteen feet. Since she was the older sibling, our mother let her have her own room. I, on the other hand, would sleep with my mother in the master bedroom, which was ten by eleven feet. My mother, in what became a bedtime ritual, would often playfully throw the covers over my head while she laughed like the Wicked Witch of the East from the *Wizard of Oz*. I always considered my mother the good witch of the South Bronx.

● ● ●

When we weren't playing outside, Colette and I helped our mother with chores.

The one chore that Colette and I regretted was shopping for food. The issue wasn't walking to A&P, Finast, Shopwell, Met Food, and other local supermarkets. We were ashamed that we had to make our purchase using food stamps. Though the food stamps were the only way our single mother could make ends meet, we feared the embarrassment of being discovered by one of our neighborhood friends using the Monopoly-looking money. As welfare recipients, we knew we didn't have much. However, being seen by one of our peers would make our misfortunes public knowledge.

One day, my mother sent Colette to the store and handed her ten dollars in food stamps. "Colette, take this ten dollars. Go to A&P and get flour, a bag of pinto beans, a loaf of bread, half a gallon of milk, and a dollar's worth of spiced ham."

Our mother would often make us beans and tortillas as her Mexican-born father had made her when she was a child. This was an affordable dinner meal that would last us most of the week. She'd use the spiced ham to prepare sandwiches. Spiced ham was a low-quality lunchmeat that had a pungent aftertaste.

Colette would grudgingly take the food stamps, and before going out, she'd roll up the booklet and stuff her hand deep into her jeans pocket. She'd conceal the booklet of food stamps as if she lived in a neighborhood of superhumans with X-ray vision waiting to expose her secret. Colette, who regularly hung out with her closest friends, Roxanne, Lori, Pat, and Porscha, would not invite her friends on such trips. She would quickly walk two miles to the local A&P, looking over her shoulder as if being followed. She'd head to various aisles and collect the food items requested by our mother. She'd look around the store to be sure the coast was clear before approaching the cashier.

This day, as she hurried to the cashier, she bumped into her friend, Roxanne. "Oh, hi, Roxanne!" she said nervously. She tightened her hand around the booklet of foods stamps to conceal them.

"Hi, Colette. I gotta run. I'll talk to you later," Roxanne quickly said.

Colette was relieved that Roxanne did not have time to chat. It would spare her the embarrassment of Roxanne accompanying her to the cashier, at which point Colette would be forced to reveal that she was a welfare recipient. As Colette surreptitiously handed the cashier the food stamps, she noticed Roxanne handing her cashier what appeared to be similar Monopoly money. Colette and Roxanne looked at each other with surprise. Then they erupted in laughter. We discovered that many of our friends received welfare and shared the fear of being seen using food stamps.

I often accompanied my mother to the store. She'd attempt to save as much money as possible by purchasing the lowest-priced products available. As soon as she'd enter a supermarket, she'd pass by several aisles. Most of the aisles she passed were well lit. The shelves were inundated with colorful boxes, cans, and bottles carrying the logos of some of the most popular brands: Post, General Mills, Kellogg, Nabisco, Wonder, Pillsbury, the Coca-Cola Company, PepsiCo, P&G, and others.

Finally, my mother would reach the last aisle of the store. This aisle was known as the white-label aisle and contained generic, low-cost, low-quality versions of branded grocery products. Unlike the other aisles, this aisle was dimly lit. Instead of the brightly colored boxes, cans, and bottles, the products in this aisle were in plain white packaging. There were no fancy product names like Alpha Bits, Lucky Charms, Count Chocula, Uncle Ben's, Pop-Tarts, Oreos, Chips Ahoy, Wonder Bread, Pillsbury Best Flour, Coca-Cola, Pepsi, Tide and others. In the white-label aisle, the generic versions of these foods had black lettering that read Cola, Flour, Cereal, Rice, Cookies, Pastries, Bread, Detergent, and other simplified names to describe the products.

To further subsidize a portion of our food bill we received government cheese and powdered milk that was distributed by local welfare-related centers. The government cheese was a block so thick, my mother had to push down on both ends of a heavy-duty butcher knife to cut through it. The powdered milk came in an aluminum container. My mother would add water and loads of sugar to the powdered milk in an attempt to improve its taste. In spite of our mother's efforts, Colette and I would never acquire a taste for the watery pseudo milk. My mother, who rarely had time for herself, made low-cost meals that were relatively easy and quick to prepare. She'd fry most of our meals using lard, a greasy substance many in our community used when preparing meals. To make us sandwiches for lunch, she'd often fry spiced ham. The heat from the pan would cause the spiced ham to take a volcano-like shape as if it were about to explode. She would place the volcano-shaped spiced ham on a slice of bread, top it with a slice of government cheese, and add white-label mayonnaise. For dinner, she'd deep fry chicken wings and homemade French fries. When she lowered the chicken or potatoes into the deep pot of boiling lard, it made a popping sound, and the hot grease erupted, causing stains on the ceiling above the stove.

To quench our thirst during lunch and dinner meals, we'd drink either white-label cola or Kool-Aid. My mother made gallon-size jugs of Kool-Aid and added so much sugar that the Kool-Aid poured out of the jug like molasses. To avoid hurting our Mother's feelings, Colette and I would covertly dilute the Kool-Aid with water to make it more pleasing to the taste. When my mother was too tired to cook, and our oldest brother Cecil was visiting, she would send him to buy hamburgers at a nearby White Castle restaurant. She'd give him three dollars, which was more than enough to feed the entire household. Most of the foods cost between ten and fifteen cents.

Colette and I attended elementary school at PS 107. The school was located about a five-minute walk from our apartment. As in many public schools, the classrooms were overcrowded, often containing forty or more students. The large classes were stressful for even the kindest teacher. The teachers had no personal time with any one student to ensure that he or she understood the lesson. Students who talked or laughed during the lesson made life tougher for the teachers. Unfortunately, I was one of the students who did both.

One of my favorite grade-school teachers, Mr. Fisherman, was at his wit's end with our unruly class. As he attempted to gain the attention of the class, I continued to talk to and laugh with a nearby classmate.

"Sloan!" Mr. Fisherman shouted. "Come up here!"

The classmates who were laughing along with me now erupted in a chorus of "Ooh," indicating that I was in a world of trouble. He bent me over his knee and gave me five whacks on my buttocks. I was shocked that Mr. Fisherman, normally a quiet man, would discipline me that way. After school, I ran home to tell my mother. I barged through the door with tears in my eyes. Through sobs I said, "Ma, Mr. Fisherman spanked me on my butt!"

"Why did he do that?"

I was silent.

She repeated the question with a stern look.

"I was talking while he was trying to teach," I sheepishly confessed. She then grabbed me, bent me over her knee, and gave me another spanking.

From that day forward, I became one of Mr. Fisherman's best-behaved students. Yet I hadn't fully repented of being a prankster. A few days later, our class was lined up in the school lobby for a fire drill. A big-boned African American woman named Mrs. Jones coordinated the drills in military fashion. As she instructed kids to line up, I sang a famous song by Billy Paul. "Me and Mrs. Jones…we got a thing goin' on…" Little did I know that the song was about a man having an extra-marital affair with a mistress. The other kids, who were also familiar with the ballad, laughed initially and then became eerily silent.

Unknown to me, Mrs. Jones towered behind me as I continued to sing the song with my eyes closed. As I opened my eyes and turned to see what the other kids were looking at, I was startled to find Mrs. Jones standing over me. She seemed as if she was ten feet tall. Her light-skinned freckled complexion had turned red. She stood staring at me with one hand on her hip. Her other hand gripped a twelve-inch ruler. "Give me your hand," Mrs. Jones sternly requested.

I opened up the palm of my hand. In one lightning-fast move, Mrs. Jones whacked the palm of my hand with her ruler. My palm felt like it was on fire. "Now get back in line and behave."

My singing career came to an abrupt end. I would no longer sing "Me and Mrs. Jones." I would also never tell my mother of the incident. I knew that she would also issue punishment once she found out why I was disciplined by Mrs. Jones.

"I WANT YOU BACK"

During the spring of 1970, Colette and her friends were hanging out on our front stoop. Her closest friends were Roxanne, Lori, Pat, and Porscha. Like Colette, all four of her friends were about ten years old and extremely bright. They were some of the top students at PS 107. As they sat on the stoop with nothing to do, her friend Pat said, "I'm so bored. I wish we could listen to some music."

"Colette, can you run upstairs and get your radio?" Roxanne asked.

Colette opened the screen door, ran up the ten stairs that led to her bedroom, and got her transistor radio off the top of her dresser. It was a white transistor radio shaped like—and about the size of—a softball. It had two aluminum dials to control the volume and tuning. On the other side of the ball-shaped radio was an open window that contained the dial information. It was also equipped with a small chain for easy carrying. She ran downstairs to rejoin her friends.

She turned on the transistor radio with one of the dials and raised the volume. She used the other dial to tune into the station. The static could be unbearable at times, so she repositioned herself on the stoop for better reception. She searched for WWRL and WBLS, two popular radio stations that regularly played the top hits in soul, urban contemporary, and R&B music.

The girls sang along and clapped their hands to one R&B song after the other. "Someday We'll Be Together" by Diana Ross and the Supremes, "Call Me" by Aretha Franklin, "Thank You" by Sly & the Family Stone,

"Love on a Two-Way Street" by the Moments, "Turn Back the Hands of Time" by Tyrone Davis, and many others. Then a DJ introduced a new up-and-coming group. "Here is the Jackson 5's 'I Want You Back.'"

Though the record had been released some time before, this was the first time they'd heard it. They quickly picked up the chorus and started to sing along. The song became a hit and was on regular rotation on WWRL and WBLS. "They sound like they are about our age," Colette said. At that time, neither Colette nor her friends knew what the members of the group looked like. They simply loved the music.

From that day forward, Colette or one of her friends always walked around with a transistor radio waiting for the hit song to come on. "They're about to play 'I Want You Back,'" one of the girls would scream as the song was being introduced. Colette and her friends immediately fell in love with the music of the Jackson 5, although they hadn't yet seen how the five talented brothers looked or dressed.

"Why don't we go to the record store and look for their records? We will be able to see how they look and buy their records," Roxanne suggested.

Colette shouted toward the second-level front window, where our mother sat watching over Colette and her friends. "Ma, we are going to the record store, OK?"

"OK, Colette. Take Googie with you."

"C'mon, Ma. Do I have to?"

"Yes," my mother replied authoritatively.

"C'mon, Googie." My sister reluctantly grabbed my hand.

I wasn't disappointed by Colette's lack of enthusiasm to take me along. I had no interest in hanging out with her and her entourage, either.

"Ma, can I get a few dollars in case I find a record I like? Colette ran upstairs.

"What record are you planning to buy?" our mother asked.

"We are going to see if the Jackson 5 songs we've been listening to on the radio are at the record store."

Our mother handed Colette two dollars.

The record store was near the Soundview project in an area known as Cozy Corner about a mile away from our apartment. On one-street block was the Cozy Corner Lounge and a candy store. Then there was a liquor store, and next to that was the record store. As we got closer to our destination, we heard R&B music coming from a small speaker that was placed outside the record store, hits by R&B artist such as Aretha Franklin, James Brown, the Temptations, Diana Ross, and many others.

As we entered the store, Colette went to the record store owner and asked, "Do you have any forty-fives or LPs by the Jackson 5?" Forty-fives were seven-inch vinyl records that had a side A and a side B with a single on each side. LPs, on the other hand, were twelve-inch vinyl records that had several songs on each side.

"Yes, over there in the J section." The owner pointed to the back of the record store. Colette and her friends ran over to section J. They fingered through the album covers arranged in alphabetical order. Suddenly, they all screamed. They found the Jackson 5's debut album, *Diana Ross Presents the Jackson 5*. The brothers were lined up one behind the other from youngest to eldest: Michael, Marlon, Jermaine, Tito, and Jackie.

For the first time, Colette and her friends saw the handsome faces of the five boys they'd been listening to on the radio. It was love at first sight for Colette. She screamed, "Michael is mine!" making an early claim on her teen idol.

"I got Marlon!" shouted Roxanne.

"Jermaine is mine, girls!" Porscha exclaimed.

"Tito is my boyfriend!" said Lori.

"Jackie is my man." said Pat.

Each girl made sure she never broke the code of claiming the other's idol. Colette and her friends continued to gaze at the album cover, pointing out every facial feature of the brothers and complimenting their attire.

"I Want You Back" appeared on the front of the album cover. This song was a big hit with Colette and her friends and would sell close to five million copies worldwide.[2] Colette purchased the album immediately. Some of her friends purchased the album while others purchased the forty-five with the single "I Want You Back." Colette couldn't wait to get home to listen to her new album. As we headed back home, she held my hand in one of hers, and with the other she clutched close to her chest the brown paper bag containing her new album.

As soon as we arrived home, Colette ran upstairs. "Mommy, you have to see the Jackson 5!" Colette pulled the LP out of the brown paper bag and showed the cover to our mother. "They are handsome boys," she said.

"Especially Michael," Colette agreed.

In her room, Colette had an old record player that had a wood veneer base and a small speaker. An arm with a small needle was placed on the record causing music to erupt from the small speaker. The old player would cause records to skip with regularity. To keep the record from skipping, our mother taped a coin to the top of the arm, giving it enough weight to stay on the grooves, so the record played smoothly.

Suddenly, the Jackson 5 were singing "I Want You Back" from Colette's low-quality speaker. Though other songs—"Standing in the Shadows of Love" (the Four Tops), Gordon Keith's "You've Changed," and "Can You Remember" by the Delfonics—were on side A of the album, Colette would regularly listen and sing to "I Want You Back." Periodically, she would play songs on side B like Steve Wonder's "My Cherie Amour," "(I Know) I'm Losing You by the Temptations," Marvin Gaye's "Chained," and "Stand!" by Sly and the Family Stone.

My mother also enjoyed the album, because she was familiar with some of the rerecorded Motown and other R&B hits. My mother, whose bedroom was next to Colette's, hummed the songs as she sat on the edge of her bed sewing our clothes. After listening to her favorite hit, Colette turned to side B and started playing a song Smokey Robinson's "Who's Loving You." As our mother listened to young Michael Jackson

---

2 "Diana Ross Presents the Jackson 5," http://en.wikipedia.org/wiki/
Diana_Ross_Presents_the_Jackson_5 (July 12, 2013).

sing the introduction of the song, she was taken aback. She went to Colette's room and stood in the doorway to listen to this young boy sing this mature song. As the song ended, our mother said, "Wow, Colette, that boy sings like an adult. He's singing that song like he's a grown man. That Michael is something else." Colette smiled in confirmation.

Sometime before, Smokey Robinson, the producer of "Who's Loving You," made a similar comment. "Michael, at a very young age, had a lot of 'know' to be able to sing a song like that. I wrote the song…and I thought I sang it! Two years later, here comes this little kid, and he's ten years old. When I heard him, I thought to myself that this boy couldn't possibly be ten years old."[3]

• • •

For weeks Colette would play her new Jackson 5 album, incessantly singing along with "I Want You Back." Periodically, my mother would request to hear "Who's Loving You." It was amazing that one album of songs being sung by five young boys could be enjoyed by a ten-year-old girl, her five-year-old brother, and her forty-eight-year-old mother.

Colette and her friends continued to listen to the Jackson 5 on the radio. That spring, another Jackson 5 hit was introduced. "ABC" became another one of Colette's favorites. It was easy to dance to and sing along with. As soon as the song came on the radio, Colette and her friends would gather around her ball-shaped transistor radio, singing along with the chorus. "A-B-C, as easy as 1-2-3, Aw, simple as do-re-mi, A-B-C, 1-2-3, baby, you and me girl…" Colette would often lie in her bed with her radio waiting for "ABC" to be played. She listened to the song with such frequency my mother and I knew the lyrics and often sang along with Colette. Shortly thereafter, WWRL and WBLS included other soon to be Jackson 5 hits in its rotation, such as "The Love You Save" and "I'll Be There." Every Jackson 5 song played on the radio would become an

---

3 "True Michael Jackson: Prodigy," http://www.truemichaeljackson.
com/childhood/prodigy/ (July 12, 2013).

instant hit with Colette and her friends. The Jackson 5 would be one of a few groups at the time whose first four singles were all hits.[4] Like a melodious tsunami, their music swept over our neighborhood. During the spring and summer, many of our neighbors would bring their transistor radios on their stoops or have them sitting in their windows playing their music of choice. Given the predominantly African American and Nuyorican population, we were consistently exposed to a mixture of R&B and salsa music.

The Jackson 5, however, began to dominate the airwaves. Colette would patiently wait to hear "ABC" during rotations on WWRL or WBLS. Since the stations were playing other hits such as Brook Benton's "Rainy Night in Georgia," Aretha Franklin's "Call Me," and "Love On a Two-Way Street" by the Moments, Colette grew impatient and asked our mother for money to purchase the single. She got fifty cents from our mother and purchased the single of "ABC." Colette spent most of the day listening to and singing along with the Jackson 5 as they sang "ABC."

After weeks of saving, my mother gave Colette two dollars to purchase the "ABC" LP, their second album. The LP cover showed the boys standing among human-sized letters A, B, and C. The letters appeared to be bigger than Michael and Marlon Jackson. The album was a hit around the world selling over 5.7 million copies.[5] Colette would play "ABC" on her old record player as if she had never heard it before. She also fell in love with another song on the LP, "The Love You Save." Like "ABC" and "I Want You Back," "The Love You Save" was an instant hit. Also on the album were classic R&B songs such as Stevie Wonder's "Don't Know Why I Love You," "La-La (Means I Love You)" by the Delfonics, and "(Come 'Round Here) I'm The One You Need" by the Miracles. We'd typically find Colette in her room singing along with the Jackson 5 record as she lay in her bed gazing at the picture of Michael on the album.

4, "Berry Gordy, Jr.," *Oprah Presents Master Class*, Oprah Winfrey Network (June 16, 2013).

5 "The Jackson 5 Album," https://en.wikipedia.org/wiki/ABC_(The_Jackson_5_album) (July 13, 2013).

As the summer drew to a close, Colette and her friends continued to listen to WWRL and WBLS on her ball-shaped transistor radio. Though the radio station played other R&B hits like Stevie Wonder's "Signed, Sealed, Delivered," Aretha Franklin's "Don't Play that Song," and "Ain't No Mountain High Enough" performed by Diana Ross, songs by the Jackson 5 were in regular rotation. In the fall of 1970, the Jackson 5's fourth straight hit, "I'll Be There,"[6] also dominated the radio airwaves. Though the radio stations played "I'll Be There" frequently, Colette wanted more. My mother managed to save another two dollars for Colette to purchase the album.

Colette ran into the house with the album clutched close to her chest. "Look, Ma, isn't he cute?"

The album had a blend of black and fuchsia colors with the words "Jackson 5…Third Album" in bold letters. Given that he led most of the songs, Michael's head shot was slightly bigger than his brothers. Colette endlessly kissed the image of Michael on the cover of the album. Colette would regularly play "I'll Be There," "Going Back to Indiana," "Mama's Pearl," and "Darling Dear." As on their previous albums, there were classics such as "Ready or Not, Here I Come (Can't Hide From Love)" by the Delfonics, "The Love I Saw in You was Just a Mirage" by the Miracles, and Paul Simon's "Bridge Over Troubled Water."

Family members who lived in or visited our small Clason Point apartment would enjoy the third album. Colette and I, who were ten and five respectively, loved the "bubblegum-pop" hits. Cecil, L'Tanya, and Robert, who were in their twenties and visited us periodically, preferred the R&B classics, and my mother, who was almost fifty years old, would listen to songs originally performed by the Miracles. The third album, like the two that preceded it, was enjoyed by three generations of the Luckie family.

---

6   The Jackson 5 was the first African American male group to have four consecutive number-one hits. http://en.wikipedia.org/wiki/I%27ll_Be_There_(The_Jackson_5_song) (July 13, 2013).

Before the end of the year, Colette bought the *Jackson 5 Christmas Album*. As Christmas approached, my mother decorated our five-dollar tree with old Christmas lights and silver icicle streamers. When decorating the tree, my mother typically listened to classic Christmas songs such as "Silver Bells," "The Little Drummer Boy," and "Joy To The World" sung by Nat King Cole and Bing Crosby. However, once Colette purchased the Jackson 5 Christmas album, the music that filled our little apartment at Christmas changed dramatically. Our family went from listening to the original classics to the more hip, soulful versions of the same songs as sung by the Jackson 5. Colette's favorite was "I Saw Mommy Kissing Santa Claus" because she could hear Michael speak.

Toward the end of the song he spoke to his brothers. "I did...I did see Mommy kissing Santa Claus..." young Michael claimed. His older brothers responded in disbelief.

"Ma, doesn't Michael sound cute?" Colette asked.

"Of course he does," our mother said as she continued to drape the Christmas tree with the silver icicle streamers.

• • •

In 1971, Colette's love for the Jackson 5 was just as strong as it was the year before. Colette and her friends couldn't get enough of them. Colette would tape or nail most of the covers to her bedroom walls. One day Colette and her friends were hanging out in her room. "I hear there is a magazine named *Right On!* that has pictures of all of the latest groups, including the Jackson 5. Let's buy it," Roxanne suggested.

Right On! was a teen idol magazine that contained pictures, updates, and fan-club information of all of the hottest R&B groups and solo artists. During the early seventies, various artists were featured in the magazine, including the Temptations, James Brown, Diana Ross, Aretha Franklin, and Stevie Wonder. However, as the popularity of the Jackson 5 continue to grow, their handsome faces and dazzling smiles graced the covers and pages of a majority of *Right On!* issues. Unquestionably, the Jackson 5 had become the focal point of *Right On!* magazine. The magazine provided fan-friendly information about Michael Jackson and the Jackson 5 including photographs, posters, interviews, and upcoming tour dates.

Colette suggested that she and her girlfriends take a trip to the stationery store. She knew it carried another popular teen magazine, *Tiger Beat*, and suspected it would carry *Right On!* as well.

My mother gave Colette two dollars and me a dollar. "Take Googie with you."

A trip to the stationery store was one that I would happily take with Colette and her Jackson-crazed friends. The Stationery was a small store on the corner of Story and Soundview Avenues. Most kids in Clason Point, Soundview, Monroe, Bronxdale, and other nearby neighborhoods spent most of their afterschool time at the Stationery. The store not only offered fancy stationery for writing letters, it also offered some of the most popular candies of the seventies. It was Willy Wonka's Chocolate Factory of the South Bronx, offering all the candies most kids dreamed of.

Mr. and Mrs. Wank, a middle-aged congenial Jewish couple who were well liked and respected in our community, owned it. Mrs. Wank was also Colette's teacher at PS 107. She was instrumental in teaching Colette beautiful penmanship.

Colette and her friends rushed to the back of the store where *Tiger Beat* and other magazines were shelved. I, on the other hand, walked directly to the glass-encased counter that contained a wide variety of colorfully packaged candy. I pressed my face against the glass counter top gazing at the delectable treats. The choices seemed endless. Abba Zaba Minis, Apple Heads, Boston Baked Beans, Charms, Sweet & Sour Pops, Cherry Heads, Fizzies, Smarties, Hot Tamales, Jolly Rancher Sticks, Laffy Taffy, Licorice Pipes, Pixy Sticks, Pop Rocks, Razzles, Sugar Daddy Pops, SweetTarts, Wax Lips, Zotz, Atomic Fireballs, Bazooka Gum, Candy Necklace, Jaw Breakers, Lemonheads, Now & Laters, and many others.

"How can I help you, young man?" Mr. Wank, the "Willy Wonka" of the South Bronx, asked.

"Yes, sir. I'll have two packs of SweetTarts, five Pixy Sticks, one Apple Jolly Rancher Stick, one Bazooka gum, a box of Lemon Heads, a Chunky Bar, one Three Musketeer Bar and a pack of Now & Laters."

"Is that all, son?"

"Oh, can you also give me some Boston Baked Beans, a Chico-Stick, and a Clark Bar for my mother?" My mother had her favorite sweets, too.

"Anything else?"

I scanned the glass case one last time before concluding my order. "Yes, one Lik-M-Aid Fun Dip."

"That will be seventy-five cents." Mr. Wank placed all of the candy in a small brown paper bag. As I handed Mr. Wank the dollar my mother had given me, we were startled by Colette and her preteen friends screaming as they pointed at the *Right On!* magazine Colette held in her hands.

"Is everything OK, ladies?" Mr. Wank asked with great concern.

"Yes, sir," Pat, one of Colette's friends, said.

They resumed their frenzied state. "It's them! The Jackson 5! Look at how cute they are!"

I received my change from Mr. Wank, and headed to the rear of the store toward Colette and her friends with the bag of goodies clutched in my hand. The girls were huddled around Colette pointing at pictures in the magazine as she turned the pages. I wiggled my way into the huddle and could see a centerfold picture of all of the members of the Jackson 5: Jackie, Tito, Jermaine, Marlon, and Michael. As they had done at the record store after viewing the Jackson 5 album cover, they all reclaimed their favorite Jackson. Colette grabbed several magazines, clutched them close to her chest, and headed to the counter.

"And how can I help you, young lady?" a smiling Mr. Wank asked. "I'll take these three *Right On!* magazines and five pretzel sticks." Colette placed the magazines on the glass counter and grabbed five cigar-shaped pretzels from a nearby jar. Each magazine cost fifty cents and each pretzel, a dime.

Colette began to collect as many magazines as she could afford. Our mother would save pennies that she gave to Colette to purchase her magazines. Colette would also use the weekly allowance she received from our father, Sloan. Each week, she would go to the store and run directly to the magazine section. She'd leaf through the magazine with tremendous speed, feverishly looking for any new pictures of the Jackson 5. Her choices were primarily based on the number of pictures of Michael Jackson and the Jackson 5 that the magazine contained. Any magazines that contained centerfolds of Michael Jackson and the Jackson 5 were immediately purchased.

Colette ran home after picking up her *Right On!* magazines, anxious to examine each image of Michael Jackson and the Jackson 5 in greater detail. She'd take a shortcut to get home as quickly as possible. She'd run from Soundview Avenue, down an alleyway that ran between Clason Point and the northern end of the PS 107 schoolyard. She'd jump through a huge hole in the six-foot-high fence. She ran across the northern section of the schoolyard where stood a fifteen-foot-high concrete wall that was used as a handball and paddleball court. Gang members were known to hang out in this area, as evidenced by the gang signs and names spray painted on the concrete wall. Colette would pick up her pace as she quickly glanced at the infamous gang signs and names on the wall: the Savage Nomads, the Black Spades. Then she'd run through our small backyard and into our back door.

● ● ●

"Look at this!" Colette opened a magazine to a centerfold picture of Michael Jackson smiling wearing a chocolate brown applejack, a popular style of hat during the seventies. "He is so cute." Colette said as she gazed at the picture and sighed. "Ma, I just love him." Colette kissed Michael's image.

My mother simply watched Colette and smiled. "Yes, he is a handsome boy." Our mother was always completely engaged in our conversations with her, whatever the topic. She listened intently as her daughter expressed her love for Michael and the Jacksons.

Colette ran upstairs and carefully removed the staples from the center of her magazines, being sure not to tear the pictures. There were magazine cutouts and small posters everywhere. She taped them virtually everywhere in her room. The walls. The closet door. She even posted a few on her ceiling so she could stare into the faces of Michael Jackson and the Jackson 5 as she drifted to sleep. She would have taped them to her bedroom window, but the grate prevented her from doing so.

She also bought large posters of the Jackson 5 that she would tape to her walls. One two-by-three-foot collage-like poster featured a large image of all of the brothers in its center surrounded by what appeared to be hundreds of smaller pictures. Some of the smaller images included standalone and head shots of each brother, while others showed the talented young boys together in various fun activities.

Some posters would have an image of Michael alone with a dazzling smile and a large Afro. The others were images of the entire group dressed in bell-bottomed pants, long-lapelled shirts, vests, ankle boots, and other seventies-style clothing. Each brother sported an Afro the size of a basketball. On the front of her bedroom door was a close-up image of Michael Jackson. On the wall near her window was a close-up image of Michael with a boyish smile, his chin in the palms of his hands, and his elbows resting on a table. Another poster showed only Jermaine and Michael dressed in psychedelic shirts, pointing at the camera. Another showed the brothers on scooters. Next to this picture was a standalone picture of Michael wearing a scooter helmet. She also had posters of Mr. and Mrs. Jackson with Janet on Mr. Jackson's knee. The other family members stood around their parents.

Colette began to collect Jackson 5 merchandise and paraphernalia. She had a set of four large black pillows on her bed, each of which had a brightly colored letter that spelled M-I-K-E. She pasted Jackson-themed stickers to her notebook, and my mother sewed Jackson patches to her jeans jacket. Most of these items contained the J5 heart logo.

Colette's love for the Jackson 5 became well known in the neighborhood. Suzie Gonzalez, one of the preteens in our neighborhood, who had heard of Colette's love for the Jackson 5, had a gift for Colette. Suzie was a uniquely attractive Nuyorican with golden-blond hair and blue-gray eyes. She lived in a Clason Point apartment across from our own.

"Hey, Colette!" Suzie said to Colette who was sitting on the stoop listening to her transistor radio. "I have a poster of the Jackson 5, would you like to have it?"

"Sure!" Colette said, though she suspected that she already owned the poster in her vast collection. Colette entered Suzie's apartment, which had the same layout and dimensions as our own, and waited at the front door. Suzie ran upstairs leading to her bedroom on the second level.

As Suzie came back down, Colette screamed. Suzie's mother, known in the neighborhood as TiTi Rosie, was startled.

"Que pasa, Mommy?" Titi Rosie asked in Spanish.

"She's all right, Ma." Suzie said. "She just loves the Jackson 5." To Colette's amazement, Suzie had in her arms a five-by-three-foot life-size cardboard poster of the Jackson 5. Though Suzie also liked the Jackson 5, she knew Colette had a special love for Michael and thought she'd appreciate the life-size cardboard image.

"Thank you, Suzie!" Colette gave her a hug.

"Wow! Where are you going to put it?" our mother asked.

"Don't worry Ma, I'll find a spot!" Colette said as she lugged it upstairs and into her room. She set it up in the corner of her room. At first glance it appeared as if the five young superstars were standing in the corner of Colette's room.

She pledged, "I will collect every album and poster that the Jackson 5 put out!"

My mother continued to save pennies, dimes, nickels, and quarters to assist her daughter in adhering to her pledge. Colette collected posters and listened closely to her transistor radio for any new album releases.

As soon as she became aware of a new single or album, she'd immediately head to the record store with her girlfriends to purchase the new release.

A new single hit the airwaves titled "Maybe Tomorrow." It was from their fifth album of the same name. Colette fell in love with the romantic ballad and learned the lyrics almost instantly. After Colette purchased the album, she incessantly sang the title track, "Maybe Tomorrow."

As she passed by Colette's room one day, my mother heard Colette singing the song through her bedroom door. She opened the door to find Colette sitting on the floor of her bedroom with her new album cover held close to her chest. She was singing, "…you are the four seasons of my life, but maybe tomorrow you'll change your mind, girl. Maybe tomorrow you'll come back to my arms, girl…" Her eyes were closed and tears streamed like rivers of water down her caramel-colored cheeks. My mother quietly shut the bedroom door. She was always aware of her daughter's love for Michael and the Jackson 5. But watching Colette cry as she sang a song led by Michael, while sitting among a sea of Jackson 5 posters and album covers, was a moment that my mother would never forget.

We'd also hear Colette frequently singing another slightly up-tempo ballad from the album, "Never Can Say Goodbye." We'd always hear her passionately sing the lyrics, "It says turn around, you fool, you know you love her more and more. Tell me why is it so. Don't wanna let you go. I never can say good-bye, girl…"

• • •

During the year, Colette continued to follow the seemingly ubiquitous Jackson 5 through various media. One day Colette ran up the stairs into my mother's room. "Mommy! The Jackson 5 are going to be on TV!" she exclaimed. "They'll be doing a 'Goin' Back to Indiana' special on ABC!" Colette showed our mother the details of the group's upcoming appearance as described in *TV Guide*, a weekly magazine that listed the shows to appear on ABC, CBS, and NBC, the primary networks of the seventies.

"Well, I guess we'll all be watching that one," my mother said to Colette. "Hey Colette, why don't I use my Super 8 camera to record it? This way you can watch it repeatedly."

My mother had received an old Super 8 camera and projector from a relative. Filming had become one of her favorite hobbies. Colette loved the idea of the show being filmed. There were no TV recording devices in the early seventies. To view a TV show, one had to watch it live. As the time for the show approached, Colette turned on our old black-and-white TV. She'd use pliers to turn the knobless dial to channel 7. The images on the screen were distorted. It was as if it were snowing inside the TV. Colette positioned the foil-covered wire hangers, used as homemade antennas, for better reception. As Colette worked on fine-tuning the TV's reception, my mother prepared her Super 8 camera to film the program. Colette sat in front of the TV almost an hour before the show, anxiously waiting for it to begin. My mother filmed the show by simply pointing her Super 8 camera at the TV screen. The show aired on September 16, 1971.[7] It opened with Bill Cosby, a popular comedian of the seventies. He played a character named Scoop Newsworthy, a roving reporter. Bill Cosby had on a tan trench coat and sported a medium-size Afro. He wore horn-rimmed glasses and appeared to have a thick greasepaint mustache and eyebrows, similar to that of Groucho Marx. Bill Cosby pretended to interview the Jackson 5 ahead of a live concert held in their hometown of Gary, Indiana. He entered the bedroom where the Jackson brothers, dressed in pajamas, were sleeping. The roving reporter awakened Michael, who was dressed in striped pajamas with a matching elflike pajama hat with a white fuzzy ball that hung from the top.

"Who are you, anyhow?" Michael asked. As Michael spoke, Colette screamed, startling my mother and me. Colette seemed to rarely blink during the show as to avoid missing any images of Michael Jackson and

7 "Goin' Back To Indiana," http://en.wikipedia.org/wiki/
Goin%27_Back_to_Indiana (September 12, 2013).

the Jackson 5. Scoop Newsworthy explained to Michael that he was scheduled to interview him and his famous brothers at four o'clock.

"Are you sure they meant four in the morning?" Michael retorted as the audience laughed in the background.

"He looks so cute in his pajamas," Colette said, holding the M from her M-I-K-E pillow set close to her chest.

"That little boy is sure natural in front of the camera," our mother responded.

Scoop Newsworthy apologized to Michael Jackson. As he left the boy's dark bedroom, he knocked over a drum and other items in the room, awakening the other boys.

The boys, who were unaware of the roving reporter's visit to their room, blamed Michael for the disturbance. Jermaine said, "I'm goin' back to bed."

"You can go back to bed, but I know where I'm goin'," Michael replied.

"Where?" his brother Jackie asked.

"I said"—the broadcast immediately broke to Michael singing—"I'm goin' back to Indiana" to a sea of screaming preteen and teenage girls at a prerecorded concert. Colette screamed as if she were attending the event.

The Jackson 5 concert was held in their hometown of Gary, Indiana. In addition to Bill Cosby, Diana Ross, Tommy Smothers, and Bobby Darin made guest appearances on the show.

There was a basketball skit that included famous athletes Bill Russell, Elgin Baylor, Elvin Hayes, Rosey Grier, and Ben Davidson.[8] The Jackson brothers would challenge the tall professional athletes to a game. They wore bright yellow uniforms like the Lakers, with matching yellow high-top sneakers. Their jerseys had the famous J5 heart logo. Tito would wear a large similarly colored applejack hat.

Before and after the skits, they performed some of their latest hits, such as "I Want You Back" and "Maybe Tomorrow." They sang some

---

8 Ibid.

of these songs in a rehearsal-type setting that Scoop Newsworthy was forbidden to attend, in spite of his many efforts.

Colette sang along, never taking her eyes off the five handsome boys gracing the screen of our old TV. "Hey, Ma, aren't their outfits cool?"

She nodded her head in confirmation.

Their outfits had patterns of the sun, trees, rainbows, cacti, footprints, clouds, and other images that ran along their shirts and pants legs. Jackie also had sleeves with tassels that dangled from each arm of his shirt. Since we had a black-and-white TV, we could only imagine the colors. The TV special showed several prerecorded clips of their homecoming concert in Gary, Indiana. The boys performed in front of a sea of what appeared to be mostly screaming teenage girls. As they danced, my mother said, "Hey, those boys move like the Temptations!"

They sang classics and recent hits like "The Love You Save" and "Goin' Back to Indiana." During the performance, Michael gestured to the crowd to sing along and in complete unison, thousands of screaming preteen and teenage girls would sing along, "Goin' back to Indiana, Indiana is where I'm from!" Colette sang along as if she were at the concert. As the credits scrolled on our old TV screen following the TV special, Colette, with tears in her eyes, said, "I just have to get to a concert one of these days!" In spite of our financial difficulties, my mother decided she would find a way to purchase a concert ticket if the Jackson 5 came to the New York City area.

Weeks later, Colette bought the *Goin' Back To Indiana* album of the Jackson 5 TV special. The cartoon cover included colorful clouds, stars, and circles. It also included comic book-like action words "varoom" and "zot." The top of the album cover read "Jackson 5ive" with the J5 heart logo embedded. Underneath there was an image of the five brothers in their psychedelic outfits. She tacked the album cover, as she did some others, to her wall. She also watched our mother's Super 8 film of the show. In spite of the blurry low-quality film, distorted images of the Jackson 5, and the lack of sound, Colette watched as if it had pristine clarity and Dolby sound. The "Goin' Back to Indiana" TV special solidified her as a fan of Michael Jackson and the Jackson 5.

As the year went on, the Jackson 5 regularly appeared on TV. Oftentimes, their appearance was signaled by an unexpected high-pitched scream. "Ma, the Jackson 5 are on TV again!" My mother and I would come downstairs to the living room to find Colette watching the Jackson 5 Post Alpha-Bits cereal commercial. They'd sing the grade-school version of ABC while spelling different words using letters from the Alpha-Bits cereal. One version of the commercial showed the Jackson brothers dressed in the outfits they wore in their TV special.

Michael said, "I'm gonna eat a dog."

"What? You crazy, man?"

Michael showed his brothers his spoon with the Alpha-Bits spelling the word "DOG." After consuming the spoonful of Alpha-Bits, Michael looked at his brothers and said, "I ate it!"

Colette loved this commercial. We could hear her scream every time it came on. She patiently waited for each commercial to appear. Post cereal became one of only two nonwhite-label products that my mother purchased. The other was Kellogg's Frosted Cherry Pop-Tarts, a pastry I would eat for breakfast, lunch, and dinner. Alpha-Bits cereal offered the Jackson 5 "Three Groovy Buttons" prize inside the box. Other Post cereals included a cutout cardboard free record of the Jackson 5 on the back of the box. Each cereal box contained a Jackson 5 hit such as "Never Can Say Goodbye," "Mama's Pearl," "Goin' Back to Indiana," and "ABC." Colette collected the cereal boxes and carefully cut along the dotted lines that circled each forty-five cardboard record.

• • •

On Saturday mornings, I religiously watched some of the most popular cartoons of the seventies. *Scooby-Doo*, *The Harlem Globetrotters*, *Dastardly & Muttley*, *The Funky Phantom*, *The Bugs Bunny Show*, and others. As I was changing channels in search of another animated show,

I came across a cartoon that showed five boys with Afros. It was a relatively new animated series called *The Jackson 5ive*.

I called upstairs to Colette who was sound asleep in her room. "Colette, the Jackson 5 have a cartoon!"

Colette ran down the stairs to our living room. Colette, who'd never before watched cartoons with me, sat beside me on the living-room floor. From that day forward, Colette and I watched *The Jackson 5ive* every Saturday morning on ABC, channel 7. We sang along with the introductory medley of Jackson 5 hits. The hit songs played as real-life head shots of each member of the Jackson 5 changed to animated versions encircled by a heart. The cartoon was based on the five animated Jackson brothers going through a variety of adventures accompanied by a character who appeared to represent Berry Gordy. A cartoon character resembling Diana Ross also made periodic appearances. Michael's character had pets that often traveled with him—a groovy snake named Rosie the Crusher and two "hip" mice, Ray and Charles.

"Does Michael have real pets?" I asked Colette.

"I read in *Right On!* that he does," Colette replied.

The Jackson 5 also began to make regular guest appearances on some of the top shows of the time. They appeared on one of my mother's favorites, *The Flip Wilson Show*. Flip Wilson was one of the funniest comedians of the time. My mother, Colette, and I would laugh uncontrollably when Flip Wilson changed into his alter ego, Geraldine. Geraldine was a sassy, funny, quick-witted, audacious woman who always seemed to be one step ahead of everyone else. She regularly expressed to her guests, "The devil made me do it," and "What you see is what you get," as she seductively strutted across the stage. As Geraldine, Flip Wilson wore a tight-fitting psychedelic knee-high dress and a wig that resembled the hairdo of Ann Marie, the character played by Marlo Thomas on the show, *That Girl*.

As my mother had done before, she filmed the telecast using her Super 8 camera. This allowed Colette to watch the show long after its original airing. As they ran onto the stage, Colette screamed. Flip Wilson welcomed each brother of the group with the Flip Wilson Handshake. This hand-shaking, body-bumping greeting ritual included four hand slaps, two elbow bumps finishing with two hip-bumps.[9] This was all done in rapid motion. When it was Michael's turn, he gave Flip Wilson five by slapping the palms of Flip's hands. Flip returned the gesture.

There was a skit in which Flip appeared on stage with his makeshift stand-up bass guitar. It was made of a broomstick and a rope, and an old aluminum washtub as its base. He playfully threatened thirteen-year-old Michael to gain entry into the famous group. He suggested new names for the group: the Jackson 6 or the Jackson 5 and Flip. Needless to say, Michael did not allow him into the group. They told Flip he could join the group if he played backup. Michael told Flip, "Move back a little bit…just go back." They kept telling Flip to move back until he was off the stage and behind the curtain. Colette, our mother, the studio audience, and I erupted in laughter.

They sang a new hit led by Michael Jackson, "Never Can Say Goodbye." The Jackson brothers danced as if they were gliding on ice. Michael led the song with mature musicianship. Colette's unexpected screams during the performance often startled my mother and me, causing us to leap from our seats. Colette listened to every word uttered by Michael, telling me to hush if I spoke during the show.

---

9 "Flip Wilson," http://en.wikipedia.org/wiki/Flip_Wilson (September 12, 2013).

"LOOKIN' THROUGH
THE WINDOWS"

By 1972, Colette's love for Michael Jackson and the Jackson 5 hadn't abated. It was just as strong as it was during the spring of 1970, when Colette and her friends heard "I Want You Back" on the radio while hanging out on our front stoop. Colette's room had become more of a shrine to Michael Jackson and the Jackson 5. Her walls, ceiling, and closet doors were inundated with posters and images she'd accumulated over the years. There was rarely bare space on her bedroom walls. Her dresser top and lamp stands were cluttered with Jackson 5 album covers. The mirror on her dresser had become covered in cut-out pictures of Michael Jackson to the point where she could barely see her reflection. Her collection of albums would continue to grow with the release of Michael Jackson's solo album *Got to Be There*. This album contained what would become some of Colette's favorites like "Got to Be There," "Rockin' Robin," and "I Wanna Be Where You Are."

The *Got to Be There* album was one of her favorites not only because of the songs it contained, but also because of the close-up photo of Michael on the cover. The photo showed Michael looking away from the camera with his dazzling smile. He wore a chocolate-brown corduroy jacket with large lapels over a similarly colored shirt. He also sported a grayish applejack hat. His Afro filled the crown of the hat so that it looked like the top of Jiffy Pop popcorn just before it explodes. Since the hat could not contain all of Michael's hair, the bottom portion of his Afro emerged like two small bushes from underneath it. This was Colette's favorite photo of Michael Jackson. Most nights, she'd kiss the album before going to bed, often falling asleep with the album cover by her side.

One day, in February 1972, Colette was lying in her bed among her M-I-K-E pillows while reading a recent issue of *Right On!* magazine. One of the articles in the magazine indicated that the Jackson 5 was doing a "Lookin' Through the Windows" tour to promote their seventh album. She sat up in her bed as she ran her finger down the tour schedule.

- January 1‒Nashville, Municipal Auditorium
- January 2‒Greenville, Greenville Memorial Auditorium
- February 12‒St. Louis, Kiel Auditorium
- March 26‒Shreveport, Hirsch Memorial Coliseum
- March 27‒New Orleans, Municipal Auditorium
- March 29‒Tampa, Curtis Hixon Hall
- March 31‒Jackson, State Fair Coliseum
- April 1‒Memphis, Mid-South Coliseum

Colette's hand stopped at the next tour date: June 30‒New York, Madison Square Garden. Colette ran downstairs with her magazine in hand screaming like Paul Revere, "The Jacksons are coming, The Jacksons are coming!" Colette's shouts startled my mother.

"What's going on, Colette? I don't understand what you are saying. Calm down!" my mother responded, grasping her chest in a futile attempt to slow her own speeding heart.

"Ma, the Jackson 5 are coming to New York...Michael is coming to New York!" Colette showed my mother the entire tour schedule. "See Ma, the Jackson 5 are coming to the Garden on June 30." Colette's eyes were filled with excitement.

As she looked into her daughter's eyes, she recalled the tears streaming down Colette's cheeks as she sang "Maybe Tomorrow." Though her primary sources of income were food stamps and monthly payments of thirty dollars for child support for food, clothes, and shelter, my mother was determined that Colette would attend her first Jackson 5 concert to see her idols. There was no way she was going to tell Colette that she couldn't afford to buy a ticket to see Michael Jackson and the Jackson 5. "One way or another, you will be at the concert," she confidently told Colette.

"Thank you, Mommy!" Colette said. She hugged our mother's wide waist with tears of joy streaming down her face.

My mother had the kind of determination that ignored the odds. When she said something would happen, we believed it, in spite of the circumstances. In spite of how much she didn't have, she would say "We can do it!" then figure out how to make it happen later. The tickets to the concert were six fifty each. However, my mother would have to purchase two tickets. Colette was only twelve years old, too young to attend a concert alone. To make the experience a memorable one, my mother decided she would also have to save up enough money for souvenirs and concession food. She estimated the total cost at fifty dollars. It would take time for her to raise such a large amount of money. She'd cut many financial corners to raise the money for the concert. We'd spend less on food. The food contained in our half-empty refrigerator, which typically contained milk, a pot of pinto beans, and government cheese, would have to last our family longer than my mother had initially planned. She also surmised that she would have to borrow money. When she was unable to make financial ends meet, my mother would borrow money from her old church friend, Mother Moses. Mother Moses was one of the elder members of the Garden of Prayer, the church we attended on Tremont Avenue in the Bronx. Mother Moses was kind and compassionate. She lived in the Soundview projects, across the street from Clason Point. She often helped my mother by lending her money. Like the Moses of the Old Testament, Mother Moses was our deliverer who often freed us from financial bondage. My mother borrowed with such regularity it was as if Mother Moses had become her personal credit union. She maintained a good credit rating with Mother Moses, often repaying her in weekly five-dollar increments until the debt was fully paid.

My mother also found other creative ways to raise money for the concert tickets. She received food stamps as a part of public assistance. Typically, she use the food stamps at local supermarkets such as A&P, Finast, or Shopwell to purchase mostly low-cost white-label products. During the time she was raising money for Colette to attend the "Lookin' Through the Windows" concert, however, my mother would return home with several brand-name coffees such as Maxwell House, Tasters Choice, and Folgers. The items were extremely expensive, costing approximately two dollars a can. Colette and I were perplexed by the atypical purchases. We were shocked that our mother purchased name-brand coffee instead of the white-label version. What made the purchase more peculiar was that our mother wasn't a coffee drinker.

Our mother would send us back to the same store where she purchased the cans of expensive coffee. She instructed Colette, "Take these receipts and return these cans of coffee to the store. Take Googie with you. You return two cans to the cashier and have Googie return one can to a different cashier."

Still confused, Colette and I headed to the local supermarket, each holding a bag with coffee and a receipt. Upon entering the store, we split up. Colette went to one cashier, and I went to another. As each of us returned the cans of coffee with the receipt, the cashier would give us approximately two-dollars in cash instead of the two-dollars in food stamps our mother used to purchase the items. When we returned to the apartment, our mother took the cash and put it in a jar she was using to store money for the Jackson 5 concert. She continued these transactions over several weeks until she had enough money saved for Colette to attend the June 30 concert.

By March, my mother had saved enough money. She flipped through the encyclopedia-size telephone book in search of the telephone number to Madison Square Garden. She tried to order the tickets by calling the box office. In the seventies, there was no Internet service for online ticket purchases. The primary means of acquiring concert tickets was either direct purchase at the box office or by ordering them over the phone. Ordering tickets over the phone came with its share of difficulties.

We could not afford a touch-tone phone, which allowed a person to expeditiously dial a telephone number. We had an old rotary phone that made dialing slow and arduous. After dialing the telephone number using the archaic rotary phone, she'd hear a busy signal, an irritating sound of rejection. Since there wasn't a redial feature on the rotary phone, my mother had to hang up and dial again. She'd have to keep trying until she was able to speak with a representative. She dialed a fifth and sixth time. She couldn't get through to a live representative. For the seventh and eighth time, she'd continue to be greeted by the aggravating busy signal that seemed so loud, it could crack the walls of our apartment. With each busy signal, Colette became more nervous that she would not get through to find out exactly when the tickets would go on sale.

Finally, on the ninth attempt, a friendly voice answered, "Madison Square Garden box office, can I help you?"

"Yes, can you tell us when the tickets for the Jackson 5 concert will be on sale?" my mother asked.

"Saturday, April 8. You can purchase them over the phone, but only with a credit card," the box office representative said.

My mother did not qualify for Diners Club, American Express, or any other credit card. She would have to go to the box office at Madison Square Garden located near Thirty-Fourth Street in Manhattan to purchase the tickets.

She explained to Colette her plan to get the tickets for the concert. "Colette, we have to go to Madison Square Garden on April 8 to purchase the tickets."

"OK, Ma," Colette said, "but let's be the first at the box office. I want to make sure we get tickets." The time from March until April 8 seemed like a lifetime to Colette, who eagerly anticipated getting her tickets. She'd not only be attending her first live concert, but her first of the Jackson 5. In the interim, she kept herself occupied by tracking their tour. On the morning of Saturday, April 8, my mother, Colette, and I awakened at six and prepared for our journey to Madison Square Garden. Using public transportation, it would take us about an hour and a half to get from our apartment to Madison Square Garden.

Colette packed several of her magazines to read during the long trip into the city. "Hey, Ma, maybe we'll see Michael and the Jackson 5 while we are at the Garden waiting for our tickets," she innocently said to our mother.

"Not sure if that is how it works, Colette. Not sure if they will be there today. But they will be there in June." Our mother tried to lower Colette's expectation of meeting the Jackson 5 during our visit to the box office.

"Thirty-Fourth Street," mumbled the barely audible voice over the train's PA system. My mother grabbed my hand and followed Colette off the train. As we emerged from the subway, shielding our eyes from the bright sun as if we were vampires, we heard the cacophony of taxi horns. When we reached the top of the stairs leading to Thirty-Fourth Street, we saw the world-famous department store, Macy's. Catercorner from where we were standing, there was a bright neon light: MADISON SQUARE GARDEN. Our mother grabbed our hands before crossing the busy New York City street.

As we approached the box office, Colette was still certain that she would be the first in line. We had arrived almost two hours before the scheduled opening of the box office. To her amazement, there appeared to be hundreds of excited girls waiting in line for tickets. They were of various ethnicities, and most of the girls were accompanied by a parent or adult. As she looked at the throng, Colette began to lose hope that she'd get tickets. The line appeared to wrap around the Garden like a gigantic boa constrictor. The line wasn't only long; it was three to four persons wide. With tears welling up in her eyes, she said, "Ma, look at that line. We are never going to get tickets."

"Yes, we will, Colette. We didn't come this far for nothing. Let's just go stand in line."

The box office opened to a chorus of cheers. Colette watched young girls walk past with their tickets in hand. "I can't believe I got my tickets!" one girl screamed. The line seemed to move like molasses with girl after girl brandishing Jackson 5 concert tickets as they departed. Colette leaned out of line, stretching her neck to look around those ahead, trying to gauge how many people were before her. She looked at our mother with tears in her eyes and didn't utter a word.

As if reading Colette's mind, my mother said, "Colette, we will get tickets. Just have faith." She had a way of stating things as if they already existed.

"OK." Colette's voice cracked in her attempt to hold back the tears. After an hour of standing in line, Colette could barely see the face of the box office attendant. Each scream of a girl who had just purchased tickets was a dagger in Colette's heart. She was getting closer but still wondering if there would be any tickets available when she reached the window.

Finally, Colette and our mother reached the window. "Do you have any tickets left?" Colette asked the box office attendant with a sense of desperation.

"Of course!" the friendly-looking female attendant responded. Our mother ordered two tickets—one for Colette, the other for L'Tanya, our elder sister, who was twenty-two years old. She would serve as Colette's chaperone the night of the concert. Since I was only seven, and my mother could barely afford two concert tickets, she'd plan to stay and watch over me while Colette and L'Tanya attended the concert. My mother pulled the money out of her bra and paid for the tickets.

The attendant slid the tickets across the counter. Colette grabbed the tickets and held them to her heart.

"Well," our mother said, "you are going to see your beloved Michael."

"Have fun!" the female box office attendant said and then roared, "Next!"

As had all the girls before her who had gotten their tickets, Colette erupted in a blackboard-scratch scream. "I'm going to see Michael! I'm going to see the Jackson 5!" She repeated this statement to strangers and other girls standing on line who smiled as she walked by and shared the good news.

My mother had made Colette's dream of seeing Michael Jackson and the Jackson 5 come true. Colette wrapped her arms around our mother's waist hugging her tightly. "Thank you so much, Mommy, this is the best day of my life," Colette said.

"No it's not. June thirtieth will be," our mother retorted.

"I can't wait to tell all my friends at school!" Colette exclaimed.

My mother took the tickets from Colette and placed them in her bra where she'd previously concealed her money. Colette was in a state of euphoria. For most of the train ride home, Colette talked about preparing for the concert as if it were the following evening—what she planned to wear, how she wanted her hair styled.

Colette had to wait over two months to see her beloved Michael Jackson and the Jackson 5 live. The wait seemed like a lifetime. My mother allowed Colette to keep the tickets in her room, and she would periodically read the tickets in amazement. She couldn't believe her mother had saved up enough money for her to attend the concert. Later that night, before going to bed, Colette read the tickets once more, set them near her nightstand, and fell asleep. The next morning my mother would take the tickets and place them in her sewing drawer at the side of her bed for safekeeping. Given the sacrifices she'd made to purchase the tickets, she wanted to avoid the tickets getting lost or damaged.

On Monday, Colette went to school, expecting to see her friends sitting on the stone steps of PS 107. She was eager to tell her fellow J5 fans that she had tickets to the upcoming concert. As Colette approached the steps, Roxanne, Lori, Pat, and Porscha were talking and laughing together. She crossed the narrow street that separated the Clason Point projects from the school and was greeted by Roxanne. "Hey Colette, how you doin'?"

Colette did not respond. She simply smiled.

"What happened, Colette?" Pat asked.

"Y'all will never guess where I'm going on June thirtieth!" Colette said.

"Where, girl?" asked Porscha.

Colette paused for effect. "I'm going to see Michael Jackson and the Jackson 5!" Colette replied in a crescendo that ended in a scream. Roxanne and Porscha hugged Colette and celebrated with her as if they had also received tickets. Lori and Pat, however, were skeptical. "C'mon, Colette, you don't have tickets to the Jackson 5 concert," Pat said with her lips perched far to the right in a sign of disbelief.

"Yes, she does, Pat. In her dreams," Lori mocked with a chuckle.

"Y'all don't believe me?"

"Nope!" Lori and Pat said in unison.

"OK, I'm going to bring the tickets tomorrow."

Once the three o'clock bell rang to dismiss the kids from school for the day, Colette told her friends that she would see them the next day.

"You betta have those tickets with you," Pat quipped.

"I will," Colette responded confidently. When Colette arrived home, she ran upstairs to our mother, who was sitting on the edge of her bed in her room. She was repairing my dashiki, a loose-fitting, colorful V-neck shirt with short sleeves. The dashiki, a style that originated in West Africa,[10] was covered in beautiful Afrocentric designs and was worn by many Afro-Americans during the seventies.

Colette walked into my mother's room and asked, "Hey, Ma, can I take the Jackson 5 tickets to school with me tomorrow to show my girlfriends?"

"Absolutely not!" she retorted.

"But Ma," Colette pleaded, "I told them I had the tickets. If I go back without them, they are never going to believe me."

"Well, if they want to see the tickets, they can come to our apartment to see them," my mother said. My mother had made too many sacrifices to purchase the Jackson 5 tickets and couldn't afford for them to be lost or damaged.

---

10 "Dashiki," http://en.wikipedia.org/wiki/Dashiki (June 27, 2013).

The following day, Colette went to school and saw her friends in their usual spot on the steps. Before she could cross the narrow street to the school, Pat yelled, "Girl, you betta have those Jackson 5 tickets with you!"

"I don't. My mother won't let me."

"See, I told y'all she was dreamin'. She doesn't have J5 tickets," Lori said.

"Yes I do. Ya'll can come to my apartment after school and see them."

They all agreed to follow Colette to her apartment after school. Once the three o'clock bell rang, the girls congregated in the schoolyard and walked Colette to her apartment.

Colette called up to our mother, who was sitting in her bedroom. "Ma, can my friends come upstairs to see the tickets?"

"Sure. Have them to come on up."

As they climbed the concrete stairs in our apartment and turned the corner to enter my mother's room, the respectful young girls greeted my mother, "Hello, Ms. Luckie."

"Hi, girls." My mother knew each of Colette's friends. "So, I hear you want to see Colette's Jackson 5 tickets." She knew that her daughter was under a considerable amount of peer pressure to prove she had tickets to the upcoming Jackson 5 concert.

"Yes," they said in unison. She reached into her second sewing drawer and pulled out the tickets.

"Oh my God," screamed Pat. She read the description on the face of the ticket.

"I told you!" said Colette.

They all screamed and hugged each other as if they were all going. They were all happy for Colette. After each of them held and read the tickets in detail, my mother took the tickets and returned them safely to her sewing drawer.

In May 1972, the Jackson 5 would release their seventh album, *Lookin' Through the Windows*.[11] By this time, the store owner had

---

11 "Lookin' Through the Windows," https://en.wikipedia.org/wiki/
Lookin%27_Through_the_Windows (July 6, 2013).

become familiar with Colette and knew she loved the Jackson 5. As soon as she walked through the door, Colette would head for the counter. She no longer had to go to the "J" section. The store owner had already put an album in back of the counter for safekeeping. Without asking, he pulled out the *Lookin' Through the Windows* album. Colette handed him two dollars and thanked him.

"No problem. Enjoy your new album."

"I will." Colette gazed at the five handsome faces on the album cover. Colette played the album as soon as she arrived at the apartment. She listened to *Lookin' Through the Windows* many times as she analyzed every detail of the new Jackson 5 album cover. The cover contained head shots of each brother in various square-shaped insets. Written along the top of the album cover was the title and "Jackson 5ive" in an orange letters. Embedded in the words "Jackson 5ive" was their heart logo. Since she had run out of space on her walls, she placed the album cover upright against a lamp on the nightstand next to her bed.

Colette had to wait over a month to hear the song performed live at the June 30 concert. On Monday, four days before the concert, Colette became increasingly excited about seeing Michael Jackson and the Jackson 5 live. She had decided on the outfit she'd wear for the concert that she believed would capture Michael's attention. She decided on hot pants that were butterscotch yellow with white lace along the sides. Her blouse would be butterscotch yellow with white-lace shoulder straps. She'd plan to wear white patent-leather platform shoes that our mother had recently purchased for her at the popular neighborhood discount department store, E. J. Korvettes. Colette modeled the outfit in front of our mother. "What do you think of the outfit, Ma?" Colette asked.

"Girl, you look so cute! Michael will definitely notice you in that outfit." My mother confidently ignored the fact that there would be thousands of other teenage girls at the concert with equally competitive outfits.

Finally, Friday, June 30 arrived. It was a beautiful summer evening in New York. The clear night sky was filled with stars. But none of them would shine as brightly as the five superstars who would grace the stage of Madison Square Garden. Colette ironed her outfit to ensure it had no wrinkles. She also decided how she wanted her hair to be styled. "Ma, can you do my hair in the pickle-style?"

My mother got approximately twenty bobby pins out of one of her dressers. She combed Colette's hair until it was smooth as silk. Then she gathered her hair at the top of her head, folded it, and wrapped it around itself several times until it was in the shape of a pickle. She then used the bobby pins to keep the pickle standing upright. If enough bobby pins were not used, the resulting hairdo would look like the Leaning Tower of Pisa.

L'Tanya arrived at our apartment at five thirty. L'Tanya was also excited about attending the concert. Not only was she attending a concert free of charge, but she'd also come to appreciate the Jackson 5, thanks to the group's covers of hits by the Delfonics, the Four Tops, Stevie Wonder, Smokey Robinson, and other artists she was fond of. She looked forward to hearing the Jackson 5 perform several R&B classics.

I was most intrigued by the drive to Midtown. To me, a seven-year-old boy, a drive downtown was more like a family trip. Shortly after L'Tanya arrived, we all walked to Metcalf Avenue where our vehicle was parked. Though my mother hated to drive, she was more uncomfortable with the prospect of Colette and L'Tanya riding on New York City buses and trains during the evening. My mother owned an old Ford LTD station wagon that was known to overheat regularly. We referred to our car as the "green monster" because of the forest-green color, the roaring sound it made resulting from the busted muffler, the steam that came out of the hood when it was driven for a long period of time, and its large size. We'd fill the green monster to capacity when friends accompanied our family on trips to Bronx-based attractions such as Orchard Beach or the Whitestone Drive-In, located on the Bronx side of the Whitestone Bridge.

After our mother opened the door to get into the drivers seat, she reached across and unlocked the passenger door. The green monster did not have automatic door locks. Colette, who was sitting in the front seat with our mother, unlocked the back doors for L'Tanya and me. L'Tanya sat in the second section where she'd be able to stretch her legs across the seat. I always enjoyed sitting in the back section, because there was enough room for me to play with some of my toys.

The drive from Clason Point in the Bronx to Madison Square Garden in Midtown typically took approximately forty-five minutes. Because our mother was a notoriously slow driver, it took us closer to two hours to reach our destination. After my mother cautiously looked both ways, she pulled away from the curb. We were on our way to Manhattan to take Colette to the Jackson 5 concert.

We drove down Story Avenue and reached the corner of Metcalf and Story for the entrance of the Bruckner Expressway. My mother was terrified of merging onto the highway. She waited so long that the drivers behind her were honking in utter frustration.

"C'mon, lady…sometime today!" a disgruntled man screamed. He gave our mother the finger.

She asked L'Tanya for assistance. "Am I clear, L'Tanya?"

"Yes, Ma. You are so clear there are no cars on the highway anymore," L'Tanya said and chuckled. In spite of L'Tanya's assurance, my mother slowly and cautiously merged onto the highway. The cars behind her honked in unison. She entered the slow lane and remained there for the entire trip. She drove at such a slow pace that cars in the slow lane honked before moving into the next lane to pass her. With my mother driving like Morgan Freeman's character, Hoke, from *Driving Miss Daisy*, it would take us days to get to Madison Square Garden.

"Ma, you should've let me drive. We would have been at the Garden already." Unfortunately, L'Tanya's style of driving made my mother nervous.

My mother drove over the 145th Street Bridge and entered the FDR Drive. The station wagon began to overheat. Steam began to emerge from the front hood, and it became hotter inside the car.

"Ma, it's hot in here," I yelled from the back. Since we didn't have power windows, L'Tanya opened each window in the backseat by turning the handles. Once on the FDR Drive, the number of insults from other drivers escalated. Drivers gave my mother the finger or yelled insults such as, "Where did you learn how to drive lady? Where did you get your license, out of a Cracker Jack box?" There were even a few four-letter words thrown her way. We heard the comments and saw the foul gestures, but our mother rarely did. She sat upright, so close to the huge steering wheel that it appeared to crush her chest. She never took her eyes off the road, driving as if she were wearing blinders. She never seemed to hear the insults.

"Ma, did you hear what that man said? Did you see what that man did as he drove past?"

Oblivious to it all, our mother responded, "Who? What?"

We were too ashamed and felt too sorry for her to explain the insults.

She exited the slow lane at East Thirty-Fourth Street and headed west. We passed the Empire State Building whose spire appeared to touch the night sky. We also passed Macy's, which occupied an entire city block. As we approached the corner of Thirty-Fourth Street and Seventh Avenue, we heard what sounded like bees buzzing around a hive. As we made the left onto Seventh Avenue, we saw an amazing site. Madison Square Garden was lit up like a Christmas tree. The buzz we heard grew louder. It was a cacophony of voices and screams of thousands of girls. Each girl screaming out the name of the Jackson they adored. Some chanted, "Jackson 5" as they entered Madison Square Garden.

"I can't believe we are here!" Colette exclaimed.

As my mother pulled to the curb, she handed Colette a few extra dollars she'd managed to save. "Have fun, Colette, and tell *your* Michael I said hi," she said playfully. "Tell me all about it when I pick you up."

"OK, Ma. Thank you!" Colette slid across the vinyl bench seat and gave our mother a hug and a kiss. My mother handed L'Tanya the tickets to the concert. "Thanks, Ma!" L'Tanya said and also gave her a kiss.

They headed toward the front entrance of Madison Square Garden.

"I'll pick y'all up in front of Macy's across the street," my mother yelled to L'Tanya in an attempt to be heard over the screams of teenage girls entering Madison Square Garden. She watched Colette closely as she walked away in her butterscotch hot pants outfit and white platform shoes. As Colette approached the tunnel-like entrance to the Garden, she turned around and waved at our mother. She smiled and waved back. Colette and L'Tanya then vanished into the sea of Jackson 5 fans.

Our mother had done it. In spite of her limited finances, she'd found a way to make Colette's dream of attending a Jackson 5 concert a reality.

"Hey, Ma," I said from the back of our Ford LTD. "Can I get up front?"

"Sure, Googie."

I crawled over the top of the seats. The concert was sure to be a couple of hours, and my mother had to find a way to keep me occupied. This wouldn't be an easy task, given that I was an energetic seven-year-old boy.

"So." My mother looked down at me and asked, "What do you want to do?"

"Can we go to McDonald's?"

"OK, Googie," my mother said.

● ● ●

The inside of Madison Square Garden buzzed with excitement. Before entering the arena, Colette spotted a souvenir stand, where she purchase J5 paraphernalia to add to her collection. With the money my mother had given her, Colette bought a J5 program, a Jackson 5 banner, and a two-sided photo album that included a photo of Michael on one side and Jermaine (wearing a white hat) on the other, both displaying their dazzling Jackson smiles. Colette surmised that the photo album would go nicely with her collection of Jackson 5 posters. After collecting her souvenirs, Colette and L'Tanya found their seats.

She sat in her fold-up seat and looked around the Garden in amazement. Every seat in the arena was occupied, most by girls who appeared to be her age. As she sat in the sea of fans, Colette thought of what her mother sacrificed to make her dream come true. Not only had she gotten her tickets to her first-ever concert, but also the concert she was attending featured her idols, the Jackson 5. After all the album covers and posters she'd kissed of Michael Jackson, she was going to see him perform live.

Suddenly, the crowd began to chant. "Jackson 5...Jackson 5..." Colette and L'Tanya joined in the chorus. As the chant crescendoed into a feverish pitch, the lights in the arena went out. Colette and every other girl in the Garden erupted into high-pitched screams. After a few seconds, a spotlight that seemed as bright as the sun pierced through the darkness and fell on the stage. The beam of light shone upon five microphones, sending the crowd into frenzy.

Without warning, each member of the Jackson 5 ran onto the stage. Girls screamed the names of their favorite Jackson.

"Jermaine!"

"Jackie!"

"Tito!"

"Marlon!"

"Michael!"

More beams of light hit the stage disclosing the full band accompanying the famous group. As soon as the Jackson 5 began to sing, there was a tsunami of girls that rushed the stage's edge. Colette, who was only twelve year old, was almost washed away in the sea of girls trying to get to the stage. Other girls stood on seats in front of Colette and L'Tanya, impairing their view.

"Hey, sit down!" L'Tanya commanded. L'Tanya wasn't only older than most of the girls, but like our mother during her earlier years, she was also big-boned and heavy-handed, and she could swat any of the girls out of the way as if they were flies. When the hysterical girls didn't move quick enough, L'Tanya lifted Colette so she could stand on a chair as well. With L'Tanya anchoring the fold-up chair with one hand and supporting her younger sister with the other, Colette had a clear view of the Jackson 5. Her eyes followed Michael's every move. Though Colette's seat was twelfth row center and she could see everything from her standing position on top of the seat, L'Tanya wasn't satisfied. "C'mon, Colette!" L'Tanya yelled. We're getting closer to the stage!"

Before Colette could respond, L'Tanya grabbed her hand and started toward the stage. Like an offensive lineman leading a running back to the end zone for a touchdown, L'Tanya pushed her way to the front with Colette in tow. The teenagers didn't have a chance of stopping L'Tanya. Before Colette knew it, L'Tanya had gotten her to the stage's edge. Colette was so close she could see the sweat glisten on Michael's brow as he passionately sang her favorite Jackson 5 hits. Colette, barely able to be heard over the screaming, yelled to L'Tanya, "If Michael's sweat falls on me, I would be so happy!" L'Tanya smiled at her star-struck little sister.

Colette watched as Michael and his brothers seemed to glide across the stage. The group was spinning, jumping, and kicking in perfect harmony. Colette and the audience screamed hysterically with every dance move. The introduction of every song was met with screams. Colette would experience a roller coaster of emotions during the electrifying Jackson 5 concert. One moment, she was happily clapping and singing. The next moment she had tears of joy streaming down her adolescent cheeks. Colette sang gleefully along as they sang a medley of "I Want You Back," "ABC," and "Mama's Pearl." Colette cried as she sang, "I'll Be There," "Got to Be There," and "Never Can Say Goodbye." She sang along with Michael as if they were performing a duet. Her tears would then turn to joy again as the Jackson 5 performed, "Goin' Back to Indiana," "Rockin' Robin," "I Wanna Be Where You Are," and "The Love You Save." They also performed the title track from their recent album and the name of the tour, "Lookin' Through the Windows."

The song had an introduction that was similar to the heavy guitar and drum-driven theme from the popular 1971 "blaxploitation" movie *Shaft* whose soundtrack score was orchestrated by Isaac Hayes. They performed the song while doing Temptations-style moves, sliding across the stage in unison and clapping to accentuate certain beats in the song. After performing their final selection, each member of the Jackson 5 walked to the front of the stage and in perfectly choreographed fashion bowed in gratitude to the center aisle, left aisle, and right aisle, and then they waved to those sitting in the upper deck of the arena. They also blew kisses to the fans as they left the stage. Colette reached out as if to catch one of the imaginary kisses blown by Michael and waved at the group with tears in her eyes as they left the stage. It was a moment she would certainly never forget.

Colette raced out of Madison Square Garden with her J5 souvenirs and a huge smile on her face. L'Tanya followed close behind. My mother reached over to unlock the front passenger door. "How was it Colette? Did you tell Michael I said hi?"

Colette had sung so much her throat was sore. She could barely speak. "It was the best!" Colette said over the clamor of girls emerging from Madison Square Garden. Colette began to share her Jackson 5 concert experience with our mother. Colette was so excited, she forgot to reach into the backseat to unlock the door for L'Tanya, who was tapping the rear window.

Colette began to show our mother her souvenirs. The two-dollar program read "Jackson" along the top in bold red lettering. Embedded in a number 5 were the names Michael, Marlon, Jermaine, Tito, and Jackie. In the center of the program was a photo of the five handsome brothers with electric smiles, psychedelic outfits, and huge Afros.

"Look, Googie," L'Tanya said as she pointed at the program cover. "Their Afros are as big as yours."

Colette showed us her Jackson 5 banner and the two-picture photo album of Michael and Jermaine. My mother steered the green monster away from the curb in front of Madison Square Garden and headed toward the FDR Drive. She continued to ask Colette about the concert. She was completely engaged in her daughter's dream of seeing Michael Jackson and the Jackson 5. "How did Michael look in person?"

Colette sighed, clasped her hands across her heart, and closed her eyes as she recalled every detail of Michael's face. "Ma, he was so cute. I could see him sweating from where we were sitting. I love him, I love him, I love him!"

She began to leaf through the pages of the program, kissing each page that had a picture of Michael Jackson. Our mother could barely glance at the pictures, as she remained focused on the road ahead of her. "Tell me more about the concert, Colette. How were their dance moves?"

"Ma, they were amazing! They are the best dancers that I've ever seen. Michael dances like he is on ice."

"He's a good dancer like Fred Astaire and the Nicholas Brothers."

"Who?" Colette innocently responded.

"They were way before your time, Colette. Before you were a twinkle in your mama's eye."

Colette continued to share her experience, periodically screaming when her recollection became too much for her to bear, as if her body couldn't contain her emotions. "They all have big Afros, just like Googie. Jermaine's afro was the biggest of them all."

"Which songs did they sing?" my mother asked.

"They sang all my favorite songs." Colette nearly ran out of breath naming the songs sung by the Jackson 5 that memorable night.

"Those are all your favorite songs," my mother said. She was familiar with most of the Jackson 5 hits and knew which ones were Colette's favorites, because Colette played them incessantly.

"Did Michael look at you?" she asked.

"I think he did," Colette said with a bit of trepidation. At Colette's response, L'Tanya twisted her lips far to the left and rolled her eyes up in her head in a sign of disbelief. "Yeah, Michael looked only at Colette among the thousands of teenage girls screaming at him," L'Tanya said sarcastically.

"Yeah, Ma. I think it may have been my butterscotch outfit." Colette didn't detect L'Tanya's sarcasm.

"Yes, Ma, and Michael sang all the songs looking directly at Colette," L'Tanya joked. Finally becoming aware of her older sister's sarcasm, Colette reached over the seat and playfully hit L'Tanya on her arm.

"How were the seats? Were you close?" our mother asked.

"Yes," Colette said.

"But I got her even closer," L'Tanya proudly interjected. L'Tanya went on to describe how she bulldozed their way to the stage's edge. Colette spent the rest of the evening sharing every unforgettable detail with us.

The next morning, Colette was reading the *TV Guide* to determine which show she would watch. As she was reading, she discovered that the Jackson 5 were scheduled to appear on *American Bandstand*, hosted by Dick Clark. She immediately told us about the upcoming episode. Our mother once again prepared her Super 8 camera to film the episode. The show would promote Michael's solo debut album, *Got to Be There*. Dick Clark, sitting in the studio audience, eloquently introduced Michael, who was about fourteen years old. "The man you're about to meet, a man of many versatile talents, not the least of which is always being a gentleman…"[12] Following Dick Clark's introduction, my mother said, "Dick introduced Michael like he is a grown man. Well, he does seem mature for his age, and he certainly sings like a grown man."

Michael performed "Rockin' Robin." My mother, Colette, and I sang the introduction in unison. "Tweed-le-dee, Tweed-le-dee…" Michael sang, "He rocks in the treetop all the day long, hoppin' and boppin' and singin' this song. All the little birds on Jaybird Street love to hear the robin go tweet, tweet, tweet, Rockin' Robin…" my mother sang along with the lyrics as she snapped her fingers and clapped her hands.

"How do you know this song, Ma?" I asked.

"Googie, that's an old Bobby Day tune."

"Who?"

"He was before your time, Googie. He was back in my day," she said to me and resumed singing along with Michael. Our black-and-white TV did not give us the privilege of seeing the colors of Michael's outfit. However, in spite of the poor reception, we could see he had large daisies on the upper portion of his pants leg. The lower portion of one leg appeared to be striped, and the other was a solid color. There were large shredded ribbons on the outside of each leg that jumped and jerked as

---

12 *American Bandstand, 1972*, "Michael Jackson—Rockin' Robin," http://www.youtube.com/watch?v=9Mm5za6Lb4E (September 26, 2013).

he danced. He also wore a vest with large daisies over a shirt with wide lapels and a bandana around his right elbow. We all applauded as if we were attending a concert. Michael then joined Dick Clark, who was sitting in the audience. Michael was asked a series of personal questions by members of the audience and he'd read questions from fan mail. Colette answered most questions based on the information she gathered from *Right On!*

A young lady from the audience asked Michael, "When is your birthday?"

Colette shouted, "August 29!" Michael gave the same answer.

Dick Clark read a fan mail question asking Michael if he had a pet snake.

"Yes, Rosey the Crusher!" Colette screamed as if answering questions posed to her by a game show host. Again, Michael confirmed Colette's answer.

After answering questions from his fans, Michael returned to the stage. Once again, Dick Clark provided an eloquent introduction, addressing the teenage superstar as "Mr. Michael Jackson."[13] Before Michael performed another song from his solo album, Dick Clark showed the *Got to Be There* album cover. With lightning speed, Colette ran upstairs, snatched the album cover sitting at the top of her headboard, and rushed back downstairs before Michael began his next selection. She held the album cover close to her heart while gazing at the TV as Michael prepared to perform.

He sang, "I Wanna Be Where You Are." Colette, with tears of joy streaming down her face, sang along with her teen idol, "Can it be I stayed away too long...did I leave your mind when I was gone...I wanna be where you are, oh!" Michael would dance, spin, and slide across the studio floor, which was decorated with large dots. In the background was a large poster version of the *Got to Be There* album cover and the

---

13 *American Bandstand, 1972*, "Michael Jackson—I Wanna Be Where You Are," http://www.youtube.com/watch?v=MFL_gYXE6Rk&list=PLPb vLpcjJM3VOASPiiC_DJiMWFdE59hF6 (September 26, 2013).

letters M and J on a nearby wall. Colette screamed as Michael sang and danced often saying to my mother "Look at him Ma, he's so cute! I just love him!"

Following the performance, Michael's four older brothers joined him and Dick Clark at center stage. Marlon, Jermaine, Tito, and Jackie were greeted by screams and applause from Colette and the studio audience. The Jackson brothers wore psychedelic outfits like Michael's. Clark asked questions about *Looking Through the Windows* and presented "Gold Record"[14] awards to the group. He asked questions about the "Lookin' Through the Windows" tour and when the group planned to tour in Los Angeles. Jackie referred to the group's performance at Madison Square Garden the night before.[15] When Jackie mentioned the New York concert Colette attended, she let out a scream that startled my mother and me. "I was there!" as if we weren't aware the fact. The superstar brothers indicated they were scheduled to perform at the Los Angeles Forum on August 26. They performed "Looking Through the Windows" as they had done the night before at the concert Colette attended. Michael also sang "Ben," and Colette wept as Michael sang the melancholy song.

Later that afternoon, Colette's attitude changed drastically. The once-ebullient girl who had attended the concert of her dreams now seemed depressed. "What's wrong, Colette?" my mother asked with considerable concern. She assumed her daughter was physically ill. "The Jackson 5 have left New York. I'll never see Michael in person again," Colette responded as tears welled in her eyes. My mother was completely unprepared for the depression her youngest daughter would experience following the concert.

She attempted to console Colette. "Well, at least you got the opportunity to see them live."

---

14 Gold records were presented to artists who generated at least 500,000 units in album and/or single record sales. RIIA Certification, http://en.wikipedia.org/wiki/RIAA_certification (September 26, 2013).

15 *American Bandstand, 1972*, "Interview with Dick Clark and the Jackson 5," http://www.youtube.com/watch?v=jas6fDmYVAo (February 12, 2014).

"I know Ma, but they're gone...Michel is gone." Her words were overcome by a wave of sobs. My mother hugged Colette. She could feel her daughter's body jerk with each sob.

Colette tracked the tour. "Hey, Colette, where are the Jackson 5 touring next?" my mother asked as she sat alongside Colette.

Colette turned to the creased *Right On!* page that contained the tour schedule.[16]

- July 1⁻Baltimore, Civic Center
- July 9⁻Greensboro, Coliseum
- July 18⁻Chicago, International Amphitheatre
- July 24⁻New Orleans, Municipal Auditorium
- August 5⁻Atlanta, Municipal Auditorium

For months, Colette tracked where the Jackson 5 were touring. Tears would begin to well in Colette's eyes as she read the tour dates that showed her beloved Michael Jackson and the Jackson 5 moving farther away from the East Coast and toward the West Coast.

August 25⁻San Francisco, Cow Palace
August 26⁻Los Angeles, Forum.
August 27⁻San Diego, Sports Arena
August 29⁻Honolulu, Honolulu International Center Arena

In the fall, Colette continued to follow the Jackson 5 tour. The Jackson 5 had reached international stardom and were touring outside of the United States. Tears fell from Colette's eyes leaving wrinkled wet spots on the glossy page as she read the international tour dates:

November 2⁻Amsterdam, Netherlands, Concertbouw
November 4⁻Munich, Germany, Circus Krone

---

16 "Jackson 5 Concerts," http://www.jackson5abc.com/
dossiers/concerts/ (September 13, 2013).

November 5–Frankfurt, Germany, Stadhalle Offenbach
November 6–Paris, France, Olympia
November 9–Birmingham, England, Odeon
November 10–Manchester, England, Bellevue
November 11–Liverpool, England, Empire

"Ma, They're gone. They're in another country. They're never coming back," Colette wept.

"I'm sure they will be back some day," my mother said as she held Colette's hand. Though Colette appreciated the sacrifices our mother made to get her tickets to the "Lookin' Through the Windows" concert, there appeared to be nothing she could say to console her heartbroken daughter.

"SKYWRITER"

In 1973 the popularity of the Jackson 5 continued to burgeon. Their music was played regularly on most major R&B and urban contemporary radio stations, and the group continued to make TV appearances. The Jackson 5 would appear on most *Right On!* magazine covers in 1973,[17] providing Colette with endless pictures of Michael Jackson and the Jackson 5 to tape to her walls and ceiling. She'd listen daily to one of her Jackson 5 albums or one of Michael's solo albums. Colette added to her collection of Michael Jackson and Jackson 5 albums by purchasing the *Skywriter*, the group's eighth album.

During the spring of 1973, Colette bought a new *Right On!* Magazine. There was a tour schedule for a series of upcoming Jackson 5 concerts.[18]

- April 27‾Tokyo, Japan, Tokyo Imperial Theatre
- April 28‾Hiroshima, Japan, Yubin Chokin Hall
- May 1‾Osaka, Japan, Festival Hall
- May 5‾Portland, Coliseum Complex
- May 6‾Seattle, Seattle Center Coliseum
- May 18‾Philadelphia, Spectrum

---

17 "The Jackson 5," https://en.wikipedia.org/wiki/The_Jackson_5#Jacksonmania (July 18, 2013).

18 "Jackson 5 Concerts," http://www.jackson5abc.com/dossiers/concerts/ (September 13, 2013).

She began to lose hope that the Jackson 5 would return to New York City.

- June 23⁻Brisbane, Australia, Brisbane Festival Hall
- June 26⁻Melbourne, Australia, Festival Hall
- July 2⁻Sydney, Australia, Hordern Pavilion
- July 5⁻Wellington, New Zealand, Athletic Park

Her hopes rose as the tour schedule disclosed the Jackson 5 returning to the United States.

- July 13⁻Boston, Boston Garden
- July 15⁻Providence, Civic Center
- July 17⁻San Juan, Puerto Rico, Hiram Bithrom Stadium
- July 20⁻Pittsburgh, Civic Arena

Colette's half-chewed cigar-sized pretzel fell out of her mouth as she read the next scheduled date:

- July 22⁻New York, Madison Square Garden.

After reading the New York tour date, Colette ran to our apartment. She raced upstairs and into our mother's room. "Ma, Michael is coming back! The Jackson 5 are coming back to New York!"

"I told you they would be back."

"Ma, you were right," an ebullient Colette replied. "Do you think you'll be able to get us tickets?"

"Of course we will. We did it before. We can do it again." Once again, my mother would not make Colette aware of her financial constraints. She would simply say yes to keep from dashing her daughter's hopes and figure out later how to get it done. In spite of her limited finances, my mother assured Colette she would get tickets to the concert.

As before, she borrowed money from our financial deliverer, Mother Moses, and saved money from child support payments. Colette and I would make endless runs to the supermarket purchasing expensive brand-name foods and nonfood items with food stamps and returning those items to the store for cash. Colette and I began to return items for cash with such frequency that the cashiers at A&P and Shopwell began to recognize us as soon as we entered the store. We'd have to expand our list of stores to raise enough money for Colette to attend the "Skywriter" concert.

Once my mother had saved enough money, she took Colette to the Madison Square box office. Given the disappointment Colette felt in 1972 when she arrived at the Madison Square Garden box office to find a line that practically circled the arena, my mother insisted on us getting up at 3:00 a.m. to take public transportation to Midtown. She decided to prepare enough food for us to camp out for several hours before the box office opened. The night before, she fried battered chicken wings, wrapped each chicken wing in a slice of bread, and wrapped it with wax parchment paper, which was less expensive than aluminum foil. She packed each wrapped chicken-bread combo in a large shopping bag, with a large bag of potato chips and several cans of cola that had been in the freezer overnight.

"Colette, if you want to be one of the first in line, we'll have to get up at three and leave no later than four."

Colette was willing to make any sacrifice that was necessary to be one of the first in line. In the morning, my mother placed the frozen Cola cans in the shopping bag. She expected them to thaw by the time we reached the box office. We left the apartment at three thirty. The streetlights illuminated our path to the bus stop, as the sun hadn't fully risen. We took the bus to the number two train to Madison Square Garden. Colette and I slept the entire train ride.

As we emerged from the subway, the warm morning sun beat upon our faces. The normally busy New York City streets were eerily quiet.

As we approached the box office, we saw a small number of people. My mother's strategy worked. This time we were third in line for tickets. However, we had to wait several hours for the box office to open.

After about an hour of waiting, Colette asked, "Can I have some chicken?

As my mother reached into the shopping bag, she found that the wax parchment hadn't adhered to the combo leaving the unwrapped food and a large grease spot at the base of the bag. However, the grease did cause each slice of bread to cleave to a fried chicken wing. My mother also handed Colette some potato chips and a Cola that, by this time, had thawed and was ice cold. Others on line looked on as Colette ate cold fried chicken, bread, potato chips, and cola for breakfast. Before I made my request for food, my mother handed me a silver packet containing two Kellogg's Frosted Cherry Pop-Tarts. To our surprise, our mother pulled out a blanket she'd packed in her large purse the night before and laid it on the ground at our place in line. We'd have a picnic until the box office opened. As the time passed, the line became longer and began to wrap around the arena as it had done during our last visit to the box office in 1972. Colette was supremely confident that she would get seats in a great location. The box office attendant opened the service window. Our mother purchased two tickets that were third row center.

After examining the tickets and the seat location, Colette said, "This was worth waking up at three. By the way, who is the second ticket for? Is L'Tanya coming with me again?" Colette asked.

"Not this concert. This time, I'm going with you." Colette was excited to hear that her mother would share in her Jackson 5 concert experience.

The night before the concert, Colette was listening to WWRL. The DJ announced that the Jackson 5 would make a promotional appearance at the radio station the day of the concert. Once Colette heard the announcement, she ran into my mother's room. "Ma, the Jackson 5 are going to be at the WWRL radio station during the day tomorrow before tomorrow night's concert! Can we go to the radio station?"

"Of course," she replied.

"Thanks, Ma, let's get there early in the morning before anyone else gets there." The chance of meeting Michael Jackson and the Jackson 5 at the radio station was such an exciting possibility that Colette had difficulty falling asleep that night. My mother and Colette planned to arrive at the radio station several hours before the planned appearance of the Jackson 5.

My mother, Colette, and I left our apartment early in the morning, arriving hours before the Jackson 5's scheduled appearance. Much to her chagrin, Colette found a mob of teenage girls already at the station. "Not again!" Colette said. "I thought we would be the first ones here."

"Well, Colette, you have to realize that the Jackson 5 have millions of fans." My mother's reasonable explanation did not assuage Colette's disappointment. My mother brought her Super 8 camera hoping to get a picture of her daughter and Michael. Colette was even more disappointed after discovering that the Jackson 5 had already entered the radio station.

My mother, seemingly prescient, reached into her large purse and pulled out Colette's ball-shaped transistor radio and tuned into WWRL. "Let's listen to the interview. Maybe you can see the Jackson 5 when they come out." Our mother, Colette, I, and other teenage girls standing nearby listened to the Jackson 5 interview on Colette's small transistor radio.

DJ Jerry "B" Bledsoe introduced each member of the group. As each member was introduced, Colette and the other teenage fans would erupt with cheers and screams. Each brother would greet the listeners. "How do you feel? This is Jermaine."

Girls screamed.

"This is Mike. Hello, everybody…"

Colette and other girls screamed after hearing Michael's voice.

"Hi, everybody, this is Marlon."

"This is Jackie."

"This is Randy."

Tito also greeted the listeners but didn't identify himself by name.[19] The Jackson brothers discussed how they had recently finished concerts in New Zealand and Australia.

During the interview of the Jackson 5, DJ Jerry B erroneously mentioned that the Jacksons were from Indianapolis. Knowing all things Jackson 5, Colette shouted, "Gary, Indiana!" as if DJ Jerry B could hear her. The Jackson brothers corrected DJ Jerry B as well. They discussed how one of their big breaks came when they performed at the Apollo approximately four years before.[20] They announced that they'd soon be releasing a new single, "Get It Together." The DJ then made a statement that would almost cause a riot among Colette and her newfound Jackson 5 friends. He alluded to Michael being "a male young version of Diana Ross."

This statement was followed by a series of hisses and boos from the crowd outside the station. Michael's brothers laughed along with Michael at the comment.

A soft-voiced, teenaged, but very mature Michael Jackson responded, "Nah, I never heard that one...I sound like her?"[21]

Michael went onto describe how he patterned his style after Sammy Davis Jr. "He can play a lot of instruments, and he is talented. He can do anything."[22]

"Sammy who?" one of the teenage girls asked.

"That was before your time. Before you were a twinkle in your mama's eye," my mother responded to the girl.

It was also before Michael Jackson's time, and my mother was impressed that this teenage boy was familiar with the work of Sammy Davis Jr.

---

19 Gordon Skene, "Newstalgia Pop Chronicles, An Interview With The Jackson 5, 1973," http://newstalgia.crooksandliars.com/gordonskene/interview-jackson-5-1973#sthash.B7eLQQNk.FiQVXXyf.dpbs (June 25, 2012).

20 Ibid.

21 Ibid.

22 Ibid.

During the interview, DJ Jerry B played some of Colette's favorite Jackson 5 hits, and she and all the girls sang along with tears of joy. My mother also hummed a few bars of the song. DJ Jerry B claimed "Who's Loving You" as one of his favorites. Colette and the other teenage girls were disappointed by a commercial break. The radio station advertised new movies: *Coffy*, starring Pam Grier, and *Scream Blacula Scream*, starring William Marshall and Pam Grier. The station then played a prerecorded promotion by Jermaine Jackson for the concert later that evening. During the interview, Jermaine disclosed that the recording was actually done at their twenty-four-track studio on their estate in California.

DJ Jerry B discussed the Jackson 5 cartoon that Colette and I watched religiously every Saturday morning. One of the Jackson brothers indicated that the animated characters' voices were not their own. This was a fact of which even Colette was unaware. "What? I'm never watching that cartoon again!" Colette playfully said.

They also discussed some of the more popular TV shows at the time, identifying Redd Foxx, from the show *Sanford and Son*, as one of their favorite TV stars. DJ Jerry B concluded the interview by thanking all the members of the Jackson 5 for making the guest appearance on the show. The Jackson brothers, in return, thanked DJ Jerry B for having them on the show. As soon as the interview ended, Colette and the hundreds of teenage girls applauded for the Jackson 5. Suddenly, there were screams in the crowd. "It's the Jackson 5!" a young girl screamed causing everyone to turn toward an entrance of the radio station.

My mother immediately pulled out her Super 8 camera. There was a throng of teenage girls in front of her and Colette, so she turned on the camera and lifted it over their heads to film the famous group. She held my hand with her free hand, with her purse draped over her shoulder.

"Ma, I can't see what's going on."

"Neither can I," my mother said as she held the camera arm's length above her own head. Suddenly, there was a feverish pitch of screams. The Jackson 5 had come out of the radio station and ran toward a limousine parked outside. Colette could only get a glimpse of them as the mob pushed their way toward them as they were rushed into a limousine by a security guard.

Girls were pulling at their clothes. The older brothers seemed to welcome the attention. Michael, on the other hand, seemed afraid. Just before Marlon could get into the limo, a girl reached out and grabbed a handful of Marlon's Afro. Marlon's head jerked back violently from the frenzied fan's pull. The security guard quickly and aggressively removed the girl's hand, allowing Marlon to dash into the limousine. The limo pulled off quickly, leaving behind hundreds of screaming fans in a cloud of dust.

Colette was dejected that she didn't get a closer view of the Jackson 5. In an effort to encourage her, my mother said, "Don't worry, I think I got it on film." Her comment raised Colette's spirit a bit. "Besides," she continued, "we're going to see them tonight in concert."

● ● ●

Later that night, my mother and Colette prepared for the concert. They'd plan to wear their Sunday best. L'Tanya, who was known as my "second mother," would watch over me in my mother's absence. She also volunteered to drive Colette and my mother to Madison Square Garden. This time, our mother gladly accepted her offer.

The atmosphere at Madison Square Garden was electric. Its marquee seemed to illuminate the entire block. Females of all ages, from preteenagers to adult women, were in attendance. L'Tanya and I watched our mother and Colette walk down the tunnel to the entrance of Madison Square Garden and disappear into a cloud of ebullient fans.

My mother and Colette entered the arena and immediately found their seats on the center aisle, three rows from the edge of the stage. Colette gazed at the five microphone stands that stood center stage. The lights shut off, causing a roar from the crowd. Our mother was startled by the unexpected darkness and eruption from the frenzied crowd, so

Colette grabbed her hand and screamed over the noisy crowd, "It's OK, Ma. It's about to start! The Jackson 5 are here!"

As soon as Colette uttered those words, the five handsome superstars ran onto the stage. The crowd cheered. The Jackson 5 would give another breathtaking performance, with Colette and every other teenage girl in the audience screaming incessantly throughout the concert. They sang a mixture of their own hits and R&B Classics. My mother, who had listen to Colette play these songs at home, often sang along. During one particular moment of the concert, the auditorium would become completely dark and the spot light would shine on Jermaine as he performed his solo hit "Daddy's Home." Girls cheered wildly as he sang the soulful ballad. They then performed more of their recent songs, like "Lookin' Through the Windows" and "Skywriter" along with Motown classics such as Stevie Wonder's "Superstition" and "Papa Was a Rolling Stone" by the Temptations.

Once again, the arena went completely dark. This time, however, the spotlight illuminated Michael. The crowd erupted into screams and cheers. Michael sang his solo "Ben" and "Got to Be There." Colette cried while she sang the beautiful ballads with Michael. Our mother, noticing Colette's tears of joy, embraced her daughter and hummed.

At the end of the concert, Colette said as she hugged her mother, "Thank you, Ma, for getting me tickets to this concert!"

To our mother, the joy, excitement, and gratitude Colette expressed was worth the sacrifices she had made to make her daughter's concert experience possible. Before leaving the arena, Colette and our mother made a stop at the concession stand. Colette purchased a concert tour program that included a image of the entire group on its cover, "J5" stickers with the famous heart logo, a green banner with blue lettering that read, I Love the Jackson 5, and an eight-by-ten photo of Michael.

As our mother paid for Colette's new paraphernalia, she asked Colette, "Where are you going to put this stuff?"

"I'll find a spot."

Colette and our mother shared their concert experience with L'Tanya and me the entire ride home. Once Colette arrived home, she ran up to her room, wondering where she was going to put her banner and new photo of Michael Jackson. By this time, Colette had such an accumulation of pictures taped to her walls and ceiling that it was more like wallpaper. Though the top of her dresser was already cluttered with pictures of Michael Jackson, she made room for her new photo of Michael by moving her Afro-pick, curlers, and other hairstyling items into a drawer. She removed a few posters from the walls and tape them to the ceiling to make room for her I LOVE THE JACKSON 5 banner, which she hung diagonally across the wall.

• • •

As she'd done following the "Lookin' Through the Windows" concert approximately one year before, Colette became depressed as the Jackson 5 moved onto other cities. She tracked the Jackson 5 "Skywriter" concert tour and grew increasingly melancholy as the tour moved farther from New York.

A couple of days later, my mother saw her daughter sitting on the edge of her bed in a depressed state. Colette was reading her *Right On!* magazine and tracking the cities remaining on the "Skywriter" tour. It was if a dagger struck her heart with each passing tour date.

Without knowing the article Colette was reading, she asked "So, Colette, where are they now?"

"They're doing a show in Chicago, and then they are headed to Detroit. By late August they'll be on the West Coast and their last show is in Honolulu."

"What happens after Honolulu?" my mother asked.

"Well," Colette said, "I guess they go home."

"Where do they live?" my mother asked.

Colette knew everything about Michael Jackson and the Jackson 5 as a result of reading endless articles. "They live in Encino, California."

In an attempt to lift her daughter's spirits, my mother suddenly came up with an extraordinary idea. "Well, what if we went to California?" she asked matter-of-factly. "Let's go see them there!"

"What?" Colette was incredulous. Colette surmised that her mother didn't understand the tour schedule. "No, Ma, they are done with the tour, it's over."

"No, Colette, let's go and find the Jackson 5. Let's go to California and try to find them so you can meet them."

Colette looked at our mother in amazement. She was utterly shocked by the idea and couldn't believe what she was suggesting. "Go to California? Are you serious?"

"Why not?" our mother asked. The two-word question would raise Colette's spirit. Our mother's sense of adventure would resurrect as she shared more details of her seemingly impossible idea. "Many years ago, before you and Googie were born, I lived in California. I have a friend, Martinique, who I met during the time I lived in French Morocco. Martinique lives in California. We may be able to stay at her home as we search for them."

"But all I know is that they live in Encino. I don't know their address," Colette replied. Looking for the Jackson 5 in Encino, California without an address would be equivalent to looking for the proverbial needle in a haystack.

"So what! That doesn't matter," our mother confidently responded. "Martinique may know people in the entertainment business who may have an idea as to where the Jackson 5 live in Encino. If so, we can find them. I know my way around California pretty well."

Colette listened in wonderment. Our mother articulated her extraordinary idea as if she'd planned it for years.

"How can we afford a trip to California?" Colette asked. "Don't you worry about that. I'll take care of it. You just start thinking about what you want to pack and what you plan to wear when you meet Michael and the Jackson 5." She made it sound so simple. So doable. There was no sense of impossibility as she shared this idea with Colette. "What do you think? Would you like that? Do you want to go to California and find them?"

Colette was speechless. Our mother's idea surpassed what Colette could ever dream or imagine. Our mother held Colette's hand, looked confidently into her eyes, and said, "I believe we can find Michael and the Jackson 5." She had such faith that it emboldened Colette to believe.

Colette opened her mouth to speak, but no words were uttered. The tears that streamed down Colette's face spoke volumes. Our mother's idea burst through Colette's sadness as the California sun burst through a cloudy day. She hugged our mother as if she would never let her go. Colette was convinced that her mother could find Michael Jackson and the Jackson 5. In spite of having little money to get to California and having no idea as to where the Jackson 5 lived, this single parent of two children began to make plans to take Colette and me across the country on a journey to search for Michael Jackson and the Jackson 5.

This feat, however, would come with its share of challenges. A trip for three to California would be far more expensive than tickets to a Jackson 5 concert. My mother's limited finances would require a considerable amount of saving and borrowing of money during the next several weeks. There was also no certainty that any of Martinique's contacts in California would know where the Jackson family lived. If, by chance, we did find the home of the Jacksons, there was no guarantee that they'd allow us into their home. There was, however, a possibility that we'd never find the Jackson 5 after traveling almost three thousand miles across the country in search of them.

Given the odds, it appeared only failure awaited us. My mother, however, was not afraid to fail in spite of the impossibilities of the task at hand. She could tolerate failing as long as she made an effort to succeed. Wondering what the outcome would have been if only she'd made an effort, however, would be intolerable.

• • •

The journey across the country would be like no other we'd ever taken. My mother would spend the next several weeks preparing for our trip to California. She started by writing her longtime friend, Martinique. She had made her home in Hollywood, California after leaving French Morocco, where she and my mother first met. In the letter to Martinique, she wrote that she planned to visit California with her two youngest children and asked if we could stay at her home. We'd need a cost-free place to stay while we were in California because we couldn't afford to stay at a hotel and didn't know how long our search would last. The following week, she received a letter from Martinique. Martinique looked forward to catching up with her friend and meeting her two children. She also wrote that my mother, Colette, and I were welcome to stay at her California home as long as we wanted. The correspondence included Martinique's telephone number.

After reading through the letter, she gave Colette an update. "Colette, I received the letter from Martinique. She is allowing us to stay with her. I'm going to call her now."

Colette was extremely excited and continued to find it hard to believe that this adventure to the West Coast would actually take place. As our mother dialed the number, Colette sat beside her on the edge of her bed, holding her hand. My mother wanted to keep the discussion short to avoid the excessive cost of a long distance phone call. She could barely afford our monthly bill from Ma Bell and was intent on saving money for the trip.

The phone rang several times, then a woman's voice answered on the other line.

Our mother asked, "Yes, is this the residence of Martinique?" She held the phone between her and Colette, so Colette could hear the response.

"Yes, this is Martinique. Who is calling?" a woman with a French accent replied. "Hello, Martinique. It's Sodonia!"

"Oh my God, Sodonia! How are you, darling? It's lovely to hear your voice. It's been a few years."

"Yes, it's nice to speak to you again as well. How are you, Martinique?"

"Things are well. When I left the French Morocco, I moved to California. I've been enjoying the California sun ever since, darling." Martinique responded.

My mother explained her plans to Martinique. "I'm planning to visit California with my two youngest children."

"Sodonia, I would love to see you and your two children. I'm sure they are as lovely as you are. You must stay with me when you arrive. I insist, darling."

"Thank you so much, we'd love to stay with you!" my mother replied as she smiled and winked at Colette. "By the way, Martinique, Colette is a big fan of Michael Jackson and the Jackson 5, and we want to try to find them during our visit. Could you ask your friends if they know where the Jackson 5 live?"

"Of course, darling. My boyfriend knows a photographer who often takes pictures at entertainment events. I will ask him to ask his friend."

Colette couldn't believe what was happening. Right before her eyes and ears, our mother was making plans to have her dreams come true.

"OK, Martinique, I will contact you a few days before we leave New York. We look forward to seeing you."

"I look forward to seeing you and your lovely children, darling. Au revoir."

Colette immediately jumped on top of the bed and screamed, "We're going to California! We're going to meet the Jackson 5!" Colette was starting to believe. My mother's news had given Colette confidence that the impossible was possible. Her next task would be finding ways to raise enough money for the three of us to get from the Bronx, New York, to Los Angeles, California.

My mother used the next several weeks to plan and prepare for our trip to California. She'd periodically review her budget book, a black-and-white-speckled composition book that serve to keep track of the little money she did have. She'd ordinarily use her budget book to monitor the families monthly expenses, monies that were borrowed, money owed, and our paltry income. To pay for this trip, my mother said that she had to "rob Peter to pay Paul." Unfortunately, given our financial circumstance, Peter was as broke as Paul.

She concluded that there'd be certain bills that could not be paid for us to afford the trip to California. To save money from her welfare checks, she decided she would not pay the rent for the months of August and September. This risky financial maneuver put us in jeopardy of returning from California to an eviction notice taped to the door of our small Clason Point apartment. She'd also need our dad to provide several weeks of child support in advance. During a weekly visit to his apartment on Grand Concourse, Colette explained to our dad her love for Michael and the Jackson 5 and what our mother was attempting to do. Instead of advancing her the child support, our father sent our mother $300 while continuing to pay the weekly child support.

She also had to convert some of the food stamps we received into cash, the financial strategy she used to raise money for the Jackson 5 concerts. Colette and I would make endless runs to a variety of local supermarkets to buy expensive food and nonfood items with food stamps and return them for cash.

My mother also called upon our financial deliverer, Mother Moses, to borrow money. Mother Moses, who was always willing to help, lent my mother as much as possible. My mother also reduced our grocery expenses by regularly preparing low-cost meals. Colette and I ate beans and tortillas with such regularity it was as if we were celebrating Cinco de Mayo the entire month of August.

● ● ●

One day, Colette returned to our apartment following a trip to the supermarket. She'd just returned two cans of expensive coffee for cash. Colette asked, "Ma, how are we going to get all the way to California?" Obviously, we could not afford to fly. Traveling by Amtrak would also be too expensive. The choice was simple, given our limited finances. "We are going to take Greyhound."

Greyhound was a fleet of buses that traveled to most cities in the United States and was one of the cheapest forms of long-distance travel.

The entire trip would take approximately three days and involve many transfers between New York's Port Authority and the terminal in Los Angeles, California. At the time, Greyhound offered an Ameripass that allowed its passengers to travel anywhere in the United States for thirty days for approximately $150 per adult and $75 for children. On August 15, after collecting the final welfare check for the month, my mother called Martinique and informed her we'd be leaving for California on August 18 and would arrive on August 21.

Three days before we were scheduled to leave, she spent most of the time packing. She searched our small living-room closet for her old Samsonite suitcase. As she pulled the suitcase from the rear of the closet, she recalled last using it in 1954 when she had escaped from her late husband. When she opened the suitcase, hundreds of old black-and-white photographs fell out and scattered onto the living-room floor. She stored photos in the suitcase since we rarely traveled long distances that required its use. The old suitcase was tan and had tears on its surface. Its weather-beaten handle was held by its original hook on one end and a makeshift hook made out of wire hanger on the other. Of the two latches used to keep the suitcase closed, only one was operable. It was sure to burst open like Pandora's box if it was dropped. My mother planned to wrap a belt around the suitcase to reduce the risk of it bursting open during travel.

Unfortunately, the old suitcase wasn't big enough to carry all of our clothing. Fortunately, Korvettes was having a sale on Samsonite sets. She bought a burgundy-colored set that consisted of a large suitcase and a small cosmetics case. The new Samsonite suitcase held Colette's and my clothes. Colette used the cosmetics case to store over seventy-five *Right On!* magazines to read during the three-day trip. In a separate shoulder bag, my mother packed her Super 8 camera, her Kodak camera, and film. She'd use a paper shopping bag to pack the Jackson 5ive Action Game and my toy robot.

The night before our scheduled departure, she prepared and packed food for the trip. She wouldn't be able to afford dining at the various terminal restaurants to feed herself, Colette, and me. Instead, she fried chicken wings. For sides, she packed two large bags of potato chips and six frozen cans of cola that were sure to thaw during our trip to California. She also packed one of my favorites, Kellogg's Frosted Cherry Pop-Tarts. My mother also packed food stamps to purchase, if necessary, more food at local supermarkets during bus stops in various cities.

As the evening drew to a close, L'Tanya arrived at our apartment to sleep over. She would drive us to the Port Authority at five the following morning. After my mother finished cooking and packing, she said, "Colette and Googie, I need each of you to take showers tonight and go to bed early. We'll be leaving at four in the morning." Colette was so excited that it was difficult for her to fall asleep. As my eyelids became heavy and I began to fall asleep, I could see through my half-shut eyelids that my mother continued to pack for the journey ahead of us.

"GOIN' BACK TO CALIFORNIA"

Our alarm clock buzzed at four o'clock. "Get up, Googie." My mother nudged me on my shoulder. I sat up with one side of my Afro completely flattened by the pillow. Barely able to open my eyes, I gazed out the window and saw the dark sky cluttered with blinking stars. "But it's still nighttime, Ma."

"No, Googie, it's morning, and we have to go." She continued to get dressed. She told me to wash my face, brush my teeth, and put on the clothes she'd laid out the night before. After clearing the sand from my eyes, I walked like a zombie toward the bathroom, feeling my way through the dimly lit room. I squinted and shielded my eyes from the bright light emanating from Colette's room.

Colette, whose excitement had kept her awake most of the night, was already standing in her room, fully dressed, as if she'd been awake for hours. She wore a jeans jacket with a J5 patch sewn onto it, a tube top, and shorts. "C'mon, Googie, get up! We gotta go!" I covered my ears to avoid the piercing sound coming from my sister's mouth.

Once I was dressed, my mother used an Afro pick to style my 'fro into the shape of a basketball. She brought the suitcases downstairs and packed our food in a doubled paper shopping bag, including the six cans of frozen cola she'd stored in the freezer overnight. When we opened the door to leave the house, it was pitch black. A slight chill in the morning air snapped me out of my slumber. L'Tanya and our mother took our suitcases and the shopping bag of food. I carried the shopping bag with the board game and toy. Colette carried the shoulder bag containing our mother's cameras and the cosmetics case filled with her magazines. As we walked down our courtyard, I looked at the barracks-style apartments. Each apartment was completely dark. I'd never known our neighborhood, typically filled with sounds of sirens, horns, and children, could be so utterly quiet. We loaded our luggage into the green monster. As we pulled away from the curb, I looked back at the darkened apartment windows of my neighborhood, envying my friends who were asleep. I imagined many of our friends and neighbors dreaming about journeys. Little did they know we were about to take the journey of a lifetime in search of the Jackson 5 and would have an unbelievable story to share with them when we returned.

L'Tanya drove onto the Bruckner toward the FDR. Both expressways were devoid of vehicles and traffic that time of morning. She got off at the Forty-Second Street exit and drove west toward the Port Authority. As we continued through Time Square on Forty-Second Street, we passed rows of porn theatres on both side of the street.

We arrived at the New York Port Authority. L'Tanya helped us with our bags. She hugged each of us and said "Y'all have a good time. Tell Michael I said hi,"

"We will!" Colette confidently responded.

From the outside, the New York Port Authority looked and sound like a giant beehive. The Port Authority was buzzing with people as if it were noon. Entering the terminal, we navigated around a homeless man who smelled of urine. My mother insisted that I not stare at the unfortunate man. She reached into our traveling food bag and handed the man a fried chicken wing and a piece of bread.

"God bless you," the man said.

"God bless you too, sir," she said.

We dragged our bags to the nearest ticket window. "Three Ameripasses, please. Two adults, one child." My mother handed the ticket agent the cash. After handing my mother the Ameripasses, the agent inform her that our bus was scheduled to depart in an hour. As we approached the waiting area, I noticed small TVs set up at certain chairs in the waiting area. To view a show would cost a quarter. "Ma, can I have a quarter to watch TV?"

"No, Googie, we don't have enough money." My mother had budgeted our trip to the last penny. "Besides, we are going to board the bus soon."

While she and Colette sat patiently waiting to board the bus, I used the time to run around the waiting area darting between each chair. My mother wondered how her hyperactive eight-year-old son would handle being confined to the limited space in a bus for three days. She expressed this concern to Colette. "How are we going to keep Googie occupied for a three-day bus ride? He rarely sits still for more than a minute."

"Don't worry, Ma, I'll tie him down to one of the seats on the bus if I have to." Colette said somewhat jokingly.

"All aboard," the bus driver shouted. We brought our suitcases to the side of the bus, which displayed the famous greyhound logo. My mother watched carefully as the bus driver loaded our two large suitcases into the storage compartment. She was concerned our luggage would be pilfered. Noticing my mother standing close by as he loaded our luggage, the driver said, "It's OK, ma'am, I'll get all of your luggage on the bus. It will be safe." We boarded the double-decker Scenicruiser bus. This model of Greyhound bus was the vehicular version of the Pan Am double-decker planes that graced the skies. Sitting in the upper-deck section of the bus led us to believe we were riding in style.

Colette and I sat together. She let me sit next to the window. My mother stored her shoulder bag, the paper shopping bag containing the board game and toy, and the bag of food in an overhead compartment. By the time we boarded the bus, the grease from the fried chicken had begun to create a stain at the base of the paper bag and our area of the bus immediately began to smell like Kentucky Fried Chicken. Our mother sat in a seat across the aisle from Colette and me. The narrow uncomfortable seat did not allow much space for her 200-pound frame. Suddenly, the bus roared and began to back away from its gate.

As we emerged from the terminal, Colette looked at me and said, "Can you believe it, Googie? We are going to meet Michael Jackson and the Jackson 5!"

My mother's faith was contagious. Colette was completely convinced that, in spite of not having the address of the Jackson family, our nearly three-thousand-mile bus ride from New York to Los Angeles would result in her meeting Michael Jackson and the Jackson 5.

We looked over at our mother to share our excitement. Her arms and ankles were crossed, and her chin was resting on her chest. She was fast asleep. The bus headed west on Forty-Second Street, eventually entering the mouth of the Lincoln Tunnel and reemerging in New Jersey. I gazed out the window as the bus rode on the New Jersey Turnpike. I could see the beautiful New York skyline we were leaving behind. On one end was the Empire State Building whose antenna spire seemed to touch the sky as it glistened in the sunlight. On the opposite end of the skyline were the Twin Towers, standing side by side like intrepid soldiers at attention. Scattered between these two skyscrapers were hundreds of smaller buildings. As the bus continued west, the skyline vanished.

After a couple of hours, our mother awakened out of her deep slumber. She had the arduous task of watching over, entertaining, and feeding her two youngest children during the long journey to Los Angeles, California. When she woke up, she noticed me holding my nostrils closed and breathing heavily through my mouth. I complained about the pungent smell of the bathroom at the back of the bus; it was beginning to make me nauseated. My mother wrestled herself out of her seat, whose arms seemed to wrap around her hips as if refusing to let her go. She opened my window, and the fresh air brought me immediate relief. Given my reputation of being fidgety, my mother also allowed me to move along the bus aisle as much as possible. She reminded me to stay quiet to avoid disturbing other passengers. Whenever I became too disruptive, my mother would give me a stern look that sent a clear message to quiet down. My mother had a way of having a full conversation with me with just her eyes and the expression on her face. I spent a portion of the ride quietly playing with my toy robot along the center aisle of the bus.

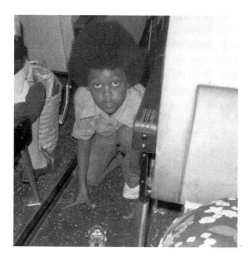

Me playing with toy on Greyhound bus to California. 1973.

As I played with my toy, Colette reached for her case in the overhead compartment. She pulled it down, returned to her seat, and sat the case on her lap. When she opened the case, magazines spilled onto the bus floor. Some were new issues, but others she'd already read. Colette spent endless hours reading through her magazines.

When Colette wasn't reading her magazine, and I wasn't playing with my toy robot, we played the Jackson 5ive Action Game. Colette and I played the game for hours at a time. She consistently won. When I'd threaten not to play any longer after experiencing a series of defeats, she'd allow me to win a few games to keep me engaged.

"Hey, why don't you guys give the game a rest and look at the beautiful countryside," our mother suggested. She wanted to use our journey not only to search for the Jackson 5, but also as an opportunity to give her two inner-city children a tour of the Unites States. I peered out the window as if I were looking at a living, breathing portrait. As the bus passed through Ohio and Indiana, I'd point out cows, horses, and other animals that grazed on green grassy farmland along the highway. Before this time, the only animals I'd seen were those on class trips to the Bronx Zoo.

Colette and I looked out the window and played That's my Car! Each of us raced to claim as our own the most luxurious vehicles on the highway. Several hours into the trip, Colette and I were hungry.

"Ma, can we have something to eat?" Colette asked.

Our mother reached into the bag containing the food and beverages. My mother pulled out a chicken wing for Colette and me to eat. She gave us a slice of white bread that contained a greasy silhouette of a wing and offered us the potato chips and cola. The can, which had developed a bubble-like dome at its top after sitting in the freezer overnight, had thawed but was still cold to the touch. After finishing my meal, my mother handed me a pack of Frosted Cherry Pop-Tarts. During our three-day journey to the West Coast, we ate this meal for breakfast, lunch, and dinner. As the bus continued to drive into the evening, we tried to get as much sleep as possible. I stretched out across two empty seats. Colette went through her nightly ritual of rolling her long hair. To maintain her Johann Sebastian Bach-like hairstyle, with numerous curls on each side of her head, Colette rolled locks of her hair on pink can-size rollers. She used the small vanity mirror inside the lid of the cosmetics case to place the rollers in her locks. After rolling her hair, she browsed through a few *Right On!* magazines before turning off her overhead light and going to sleep.

Our mother, unfortunately, rarely got a good night's sleep. She had limited room to move. The seat barely reclined, so she had to sleep in an upright position. Nevertheless, she sacrificed her comfort for the chance to bring her daughter face-to-face with Michael Jackson and the Jackson 5.

We transferred to another Greyhound bus at a terminal in Chicago, Illinois. As before, my mother watched the bus driver load our bags onto the next bus to be sure our belongings made it through to our final destination. She then inquired of the bus driver the time of our departure. After he disclosed that the bus would leave in forty-five minutes, our mother took us outside the depot where she found a small grocery store. She used her food stamps to purchase food and snacks for the remainder of our trip.

After we boarded the bus, Colette noticed a girl about her age sitting in a seat behind our mother. Like us, the young girl and her family had transferred from bus to bus since boarding at the New York Port Authority. Before the bus pulled away from the gate, Colette struck up a conversation with the girl. "Are you heading to California?" Colette asked.

"Yes, we are," the girl said.

Seeing how congenial the girl was, Colette introduced herself, and the girl said, "Hi, Colette. My name is Sharon. Sharon Parker." Colette introduced me to Sharon. "This is my little brother, Googie."

Sharon grinned after hearing my name. "Wow, Googie, I've never seen a 'fro that big! How do you take care of it?"

"Mommy picks it for me." I said.

Sharon then introduced Colette and me to her brother, Lincoln. Sharon was a gregarious and articulate teenage girl with a beautiful bright smile. She was from Manhattan, New York, and like Colette, was thirteen years old. Her grandmother, Susie Parker, accompanied Sharon and Lincoln on the bus ride to the West Coast.

Colette and Sharon immediately hit it off. They sat next to each other talking for hours at a time. Colette removed her cosmetics case from the overhead and opened it. Sharon was shocked to see how many magazines Colette had packed.

Colette asked, "Do you like the Jackson 5?"

"Do I?" Sharon responded incredulously. "Of course!"

"Well, I love Michael," Colette said as she held a *Right On!* magazine with Michael's picture on the cover. She sighed as if referring to a long-lost love.

"I love Jermaine," Sharon said. "Last year, I went to the 'Lookin' Through the Windows' concert at Madison Square Garden."

"Oh my gosh, I was there, too!" Colette exclaimed. They shared their concert experiences, singing a medley of Jackson 5 songs performed during the concert. Sharon and Colette had a lot in common.

As Colette read her magazine, she asked, "Where are you and your family going, Sharon?"

"We are heading to California. We're going to Disneyland." They were heading to Anaheim to meet five superstars of their own. Mickey, Minnie, Goofy, Donald, and Pluto. "How about you, Colette? Where are you and your family going?" Sharon asked.

"We're going to California, too."

"Who are you going to see? Family?" Sharon asked.

Without hesitation, Colette said, "We are going to California to meet Michael Jackson and the Jackson 5." Colette then read her magazine as if her response to Sharon was not out of the ordinary.

Sharon, suspecting she'd misheard Colette, said, "What did you say, Colette?"

"We are going to California to meet the Jackson 5," Colette repeated.

Sharon was in disbelief. "In concert?"

"No," Colette said, fully aware of the Jackson 5 concert schedule.

"Do you know them personally?" Sharon asked.

"No."

"Well, do you know where they live?"

"No. But we are going to meet them."

Sharon looked perplexed.

"My mother is going to find them for me." As one catching a cold from another, our mother's infectious faith caused Colette to believe that she would meet the Jackson 5 in spite of the odds. Colette shared the purpose of our trip with Sharon as if our meeting with the Jackson 5 were already arranged.

"Well, good luck," Sharon replied. Though Sharon suspected she had a better chance of meeting Mickey, she never discouraged Colette. She was impressed by Colette's ambitious quest to meet Michael Jackson and the Jackson 5.

• • •

The bus passed through Kansas. "Hey, Ma, we are in Kansas. Isn't that were you were born?"

"Yes, Googie. In Junction City, Kansas." She told Colette and me stories of how poor her family was. She also shared how she and her nine siblings manage to have fun in spite of their economic situation. In spite of our own economic circumstances, we too were enjoying our cross-country journey to California. The bus passed through Colorado whose beautiful mountains seemed to kiss the pristine white clouds in the clear blue sky. I'd only seen such beauty illustrated in books. Colette and I were so mesmerized by the picturesque scenery that we spent more of our time gazing out the bus window. We transferred to another bus in Denver, Colorado, that took us to New Mexico. As the Greyhound bus rumbled through the barren desserts of New Mexico, Colette, Sharon, Lincoln, and I spent hours playing the Jackson 5ive Action Game.

Following a stop in Albuquerque the bus headed for Arizona. After miles of driving along the desert, we passed through Sedona, a uniquely beautiful area. The mountains had the most unique shapes and colors I'd ever seen. In the distance I noticed a mountain whose flat top gave it the appearance of a giant ceremonial altar. The beautiful reddish color of rocks and dirt made me feel as if I'd left earth and arrived on Mars.

Several hours later the bus pulled into a depot in the beautiful city of Phoenix, Arizona. Sharon's grandmother noticed an all-you-can-eat pancake house several blocks away. She took Sharon and Lincoln to the pancake house for breakfast.

"Can we go, Ma?" Colette asked.

"No, Colette. We have to use these food stamps to buy a few things at that local grocery store over there." Our mother pointed to a store about a block away. "And I don't want us to walk too far away from the bus depot." Our mother did not have enough money to spend on pancakes, and she was certain the pancake house did not accept food stamps.

We returned from the small grocery store with a few food items. Suddenly the bus driver shouted, "All aboard!" This layover was far shorter than the others. As we boarded the bus and returned to our seats, Colette turned to our mother and asked, "What about Sharon and her family, Ma?" Our mother ran to the front of the bus and said to the bus driver, "Sir, there was a family on this bus, and I believe they are still at the pancake house several blocks away."

"Well, ma'am, they'll have to take the next bus. We have to stay on schedule if we are going to arrive in California on time," the bus driver said. He pulled the large silver lever to close the door. As the bus passed by the pancake house, we could see Sharon, Lincoln, and Grandma Susie eating stacks of pancakes in sheer ecstasy.

"Well, I'm glad they are enjoying those pancakes now, because they are going to be pretty mad later when they realize they missed the bus." Our mother then turned to Colette and said, "I'm so sorry, Colette. It looked like you and Sharon were becoming close friends."

Colette pulled a small piece of paper out of her pocket. "It's OK, Ma. I have Sharon's address." As fate would have it, Sharon and Colette exchanged addresses and pledged to become pen pals during the previous bus stop in Albuquerque.

The Greyhound bus left Phoenix, traveling down a highway that had barren land on each side with a mountainous backdrop. Like an oasis emerging from a desert, palm trees and lush green bushes began to appear. We had entered California.

The bus made a brief stop in Anaheim, where Colette's new friend and her family were scheduled to exit the bus for Disneyland. After the brief stop in Anaheim, the driver informed us and the other passengers that the next stop was Los Angeles. As soon as Colette heard the bus driver, she screamed, which startled all the passengers on the bus. Our mother apologized to the passengers for Colette's outburst.

We saw lovely homes fenced by tall deep green Italian Cypress trees. "Look Ma, that house has its own pool!" I found it hard to believe that most of the houses we passed had private pools. We frequented the Bronxdale public pool.

In the distance, on each side of the freeway beyond the beautiful palm trees, were tall buildings in the middle of metropolitan areas. There appeared to be more cars on the freeways and streets of California than there were in New York City. It was as if every resident of California owned a vehicle.

We finally arrived in Los Angeles. The city was beautiful. The luxuriant green leaves of the towering palm trees rhythmically swayed in the California breeze. The streets were immaculate. Men, women, and children wore colorful shorts, T-shirts, and tanks tops exposing their skin that had been bronzed by the radiant California sun. Everyone was smiling. They all seemed happy and carefree, as if they didn't have a concern in the world.

As I looked out the Greyhound bus window and gazed onto the clean streets and smiling faces, I thought, *This is what heaven must be like.* This truly was the City of Angels. As the bus pulled into the depot, our mother said, "Well, we're here!" She had given us an opportunity to see parts of the United States we'd only read about in books. Colette and I enjoyed the trip immensely. We'd taken a beautiful journey that took us through the farmlands, mountains, and deserts of our country. Little did we know that the journey was just beginning.

Colette and I anxiously got off the bus. Colette grabbed her cosmetics case full of magazines. I carried the shopping bag containing the Jackson 5ive Action Game and the robot. Our mother carried the shopping bag that contained a small amount of food and one warm can of cola that remained following the three-day cross-country trip. We waited at the side of the bus while the driver unloaded our luggage.

As Colette and I assisted our mother in carrying the two suitcases inside the terminal, we heard a woman call with a French accent, "Sodonia, darling!" An elegant woman emerged from the crowd. From a distance, she resembled Lena Horne. She ran toward our mother, kissed her on both cheeks, and gave her a bear-like hug. She had flawless skin, short jet-black hair that looked wet, a statuesque physique, and a dazzling smile. She wore a sheer white blouse, black fitted pants that flared at the end of each leg, black shoes with a cluster of rhinestones on the toe, and sunglasses that she draped over the top of her head as she spoke with my mother. She was full of life and energy. "And who are these two beautiful children?" Martinique asked.

"This is my daughter Colette."

Martinique kissed Colette on each cheek. "And who, pray tell, is this handsome little devil?" Martinique asked.

"That's my youngest child, Googie."

"Ah, Googie. I love that name!" she said with her French accent. I'd never heard my nickname sound so melodious. She articulated my nickname so it no longer sounded like the name of a character in a Hanna-Barbera cartoon. She gently placed her hands on my shoulders, leaned down, and kissed me on each cheek. Her ruby red lipstick left perfectly shaped kiss marks on my cheeks. Martinique would have seen me blushing if it weren't for my dark-chocolate complexion. "Did you have a fun ride on the bus, Googie?" this beautiful congenial woman asked.

I opened my mouth to answer, but couldn't utter words. She simply smiled. Struck by her beauty, I immediately had a crush. With her ebullient personality, French accent, beauty, and glamour, she was perfect for California. She personified a glamorous Hollywood movie star.

"George, darling, can you help them with their bags?" George was Martinique's boyfriend. He was a tall, well-built dark-skinned man. With the exception of his height, he resembled my father. "This is George." Martinique introduced her boyfriend to our mother. "Hello, Sodonia, Martinque has told me a lot about you."

"All good I hope."

"Of course," George replied. He loaded our bags in their car, and we drove to Martinique's home in Hollywood. We passed through the beautiful city of Los Angeles and drove on a highway that had more lanes than those in New York City. Then we ascended a series of steep hills. Nestled in the hills were beautiful homes whose streets were lined with palm trees. The home of Martinique and her boyfriend sat on a cliff overlooking the city of Los Angeles. It had floor-to-ceiling windows that allowed the sun to provide natural warmth and light. The living-room walls and furniture were as white as snow. As I sat on the soft couch, it was as if I was sitting on a cloud. Martinique's furniture did not have the uncomfortable plastic covering that was wrapped around the living-room furniture in our Clason Point apartment. The living-room table and other accents were made from glass, so the sun's rays were re-flected throughout the home.

Noticing that I'd already sat down on the couch, my mother in-structed, "Googie, don't touch anything until you wash your hands."

"Don't worry Sodonia, he'll be fine." Martinique came to my defense.

My mother knew better than that. She had seen me leave finger-prints over our furniture and walls. My fingerprints would be easy to identify on Martinique's stark-white furniture and walls.

Martinique showed us to our bedrooms later that evening. For the first time in three days, our mother would get some well-deserved rest.

• • •

During our first week at Martinique's home, we had no news about whether any of George's contacts knew the home address of the Jackson 5. George tried to contact his friend, Larry Johnson, who had photo-graphed a few Hollywood stars. Unfortunately, Larry was on assignment out of town and wouldn't return to California for at least a week.

After days of waiting for information from George, our mother de-vised a way to occupy the time. One morning my mother asked Colette, "Didn't you tell me that *Right On!* describes where the Jackson 5 went to school?"

"Yes, Ma." Colette got her magazines. She shuffled through until she found several articles that mentioned the schools attended by the

Jackson brothers. "Here it is! Right here, Ma!" Colette pointed to a picture and description in her magazine.

"Well, until we can find their house, why don't we visit where they attend school?"

Colette was elated by the idea. The next morning we prepared to venture out to tour schools attended by the Jackson 5 and other J5 landmarks. Our mother, familiar with the weather in California after living there for a few years, packed clothes that were appropriate for our tour. I wore denim shorts that went to the knee, a white V-neck T-shirt, and Super Pro-Ked sneakers. Before leaving Martinique's home, my mother had the arduous task of styling my Afro with a pick.

Colette wore a green-and-white patterned sundress. The white accents on her dress match her patent-leather white sandals. As was the style in the seventies, the dress ended high on her thighs. She also sported her curly hairstyle, her hair parted in the middle. She used white flower barrettes on each side of her head to hold her hair in place. Our mother wore a pink-and-white sundress that ended at her knees, and white sandals.

We took a series of local buses to Hollywood, where we visited the Gardner Street Elementary School. According to Colette's magazines, Michael Jackson attended the sixth grade there when he first arrived in California.[23] As we walked around the building, I said, "Hey, Colette. This looks like PS 107." Colette agreed that it resembled the public school we attended in the South Bronx. There was one exception, however. The windows of the Gardner Street Elementary School had no grates. Colette explained to us, based on articles she'd read, that Michael attended the school for several months until the release of the *Diana Ross Presents the Jackson 5*. The debut album made Michael an instant superstar, making it difficult for him to attend public school. Michael received home tutoring for some time after becoming famous.[24]

---

23 "Michael Jackson's Name on Display Again at Gardner Elementary School Auditorium," http://www.lausd.k12.ca.us/Gardner_EL/Site/Welcome_files/ MICHAELJACKSON%20LAUSD%20Press%20Release.pdf (September 21, 2013).

24 Ibid.

The following day, we boarded a local bus that took us down Sunset Boulevard to North Saint Vicente Boulevard. From there we walked to the West Hollywood Park. Based on Colette's knowledge of all things Jackson 5, it was her understanding that members of the Jackson 5 frequently visited the park. As we looked around the park, we couldn't believe our eyes. Surrounding the park were beautiful green trees, some of which were blooming with white and red flowers. I picked about a dozen flowers and handed them to my mother, who taught me that women love bouquets.

In spite of my chivalrous attempt, my mother didn't feel comfortable with her eight-year-old son picking flowers from the perfectly manicured trees. "Thank you, Googie, but don't pick anymore flowers. We don't want to damage the plants and trees in this beautiful park."

As Colette walked among the beautifully landscaped park, she discovered a tree that contained the carved initials M and what appeared to be a J. Colette showed us the carving and said, "I wonder if Michael or Marlon was here."

We were amazed by the park's Olympic-size swimming pool. The sun's rays brilliantly reflected off its rippling water. Through the clear water we saw the pool's turquoise tile bottom. This pool dwarfed the murky Bronxdale community pool shared by those who lived in Bronxdale, Clason Point, Soundview, and other neighborhood projects. As we continued to tour the park we saw tennis courts with white borderlines and white nets. In the big park between the Soundview and Clason Point projects, there were no tennis courts. Instead, there were handball courts. Three twenty-five-foot-wide by twenty-foot-high concrete walls. Painted along the concrete walls and ground were weathered yellow borderlines. Instead of tennis racquets, players used the palms of their hands to hit a small Spalding ball against the concrete wall.

West Hollywood Park also had basketball courts. Each court was built on a smooth concrete surface with white boundary and foul shot lines. Each basketball rim held a pristine white net. Colette walked across a basketball court, as if it were hallowed ground, wondering if

Jackie, Tito, Jermaine, or Marlon had played there just days before. As I walked across the court and gazed at the fresh white nets hanging from each rim, I compared it to the basketball courts at home. The courts in our neighborhood park were built on uneven concrete. Over time, cracks in the concrete had developed, allowing grass to emerge in various areas on the court. Not only didn't the basketball rims contain nets, allowing us to hear a "swoosh" after a jump shot, some courts didn't contain a rim or backboard.

The following day, Colette showed our mother a page in her *Right On!* magazine. "See Ma, according to this, Jermaine and Marlon attended Fairfax High School."[25] We boarded another series of buses that took us to Melrose Avenue. As the bus approached the corner of North Fairfax and Melrose, we were amazed at what we saw.

"That's where they go to high school? It's beautiful!" Colette said.

"It looks more like a Hollywood Studio," Our mother said. Fairfax High School, unlike Stevenson, Lehman, Truman, or other high schools in the Bronx, had the appearance of a college campus. The campus occupied more than a city block. The marquee read, FAIRFAX HIGH SCHOOL in bold red letters on a yellow background. Below that it said, FAIRFAX COMMUNITY ADULT SCHOOL in bold but smaller black letters on a white background.

There was a huge parking lot, with signs for the reserved spots that read, PRINCIPAL and ASSISTANT PRINCIPAL. However, the majority of the parking spots were not labeled. "Who are all these parking spots for?" Colette asked as she looked over the three-foot high gate surrounding the parking lot area.

"Probably the students," our mother said.

"No way! The students drive themselves to school? The students have cars?" Colette asked incredulously.

Colette and I looked at each other amazed at the idea of students driving themselves to school. In our neighborhood, most high school students

---

25 "Fairfax High School, Notable Alumni," http://www.fairfaxhs.org/apps/pages/index.jsp?uREC_ID=33840&type=d&pREC_ID=33142 (February 27, 2014).

either walked or road the Bx 27, Bx 5, or another bus to school. Others had to take a bus and a train to get to their high school. Well-manicured bushes and small Christmas-like pine trees surrounded the Fairfax High School buildings. The trees and bushes were of the deepest green that I'd ever seen. In other areas on the school grounds stood tall Italian cypress trees that seemed to reach the sky. One building resembled an office building. Colette approached the front of the building and walked up a series of steps to the locked glass doors. Our mother filmed Colette posing on top of a wall in front of the school building that was approximately six feet high. Colette, wearing white hot pants with a jacket, a tube top with a large sparkling question mark, and matching white sandals, waved at the camera and pointed to the metal block letters that read, FAIRFAX HIGH SCHOOL.

As we walked back across Fairfax High School to the bus stop, I saw Colette gazing at certain areas of the campus. "What are you staring at Colette?"

"I wonder if Jermaine and Marlon sat in that area near the school stairs during recess or sat on the wall that I posed on where Mommy took pictures of me." Colette walked across the campus as if it were sacrosanct, wondering whether Jermaine and Marlon walked along the same path, staring at the pathway as if she could see the footprints of the Jackson 5.

• • •

At the beginning of our second week in California, our mother asked Martinique whether George was having any luck getting the home address of the Jackson 5. George was seldom at the house.

"Yes, Sodonia. George gave me the telephone number of his friend Larry, who is a paparazzo and often takes pictures of movie stars. Here's his number, you can give him a call to see if he knows anything or anyone who may know the home address of the Jackson 5."

"Thank you so much, Martinique. This will mean a lot to Colette." Later that evening, our mother called Larry's home. His wife, Elizabeth, informed her that he was out of town and would return the following week.

A couple of days later my mother and Martinique had a disagreement. Though I was only eight years old, and unaware of the details of their dispute, I could sense the tension between them. As tensions continued to mount, my mother no longer felt comfortable at Martinique's home and decided to find somewhere else for us to stay. She began to pack our clothes and other belongings.

"Where are we going, Ma?" Colette asked.

"We are going to leave tomorrow morning," our mother said without looking at Colette. She continued to pack.

"Where are we going to go? Where are we going to stay?" Colette asked. Our mother had similar questions racing through her mind. She budgeted the trip based on the assumption that we would be staying with Martinique. We didn't have enough cash to stay at a hotel. We had consumed all the food she'd packed for our three-day bus ride from New York City to Los Angeles. We'd also begun to run out of cash and food stamps. We had nowhere else to stay. She knew no one, outside of Martinique, who would allow us to stay with them as we searched for the Jackson 5.

Given the circumstances, it would have been reasonable for our mother to use the little we had left to get us back home. However, she'd come too far to give up on her goal of having her daughter meet Michael Jackson and the Jackson 5. The next morning, we helped our mother move our luggage near the front door.

"George can drive you wherever you need to go," Martinique said.

"No thank you, Martinique. I'll just call a cab."

Approximately fifteen minutes later, the cab arrived. Colette and I helped our mother pack our luggage in the cab. Martinique walked us to the curb, kissing Colette and me on both cheeks as she had done when we first met. Our mother and Martinique shook hands.

"Take care of yourself, Martinique," our mother said.

"You too," Martinique replied.

As we got into the cab, the cab driver asked, "Where to, ma'am?" Our mother replied, "Take us to the nearest shelter."

• • •

The scenery changed dramatically as the cab drove us from the beautiful lush Hollywood Hills to a back-street area in the city of Los Angeles. Smaller lifeless trees replaced the deep-green skyscraping Italian Cypress trees. Concrete streets littered with garbage replaced the well-manicured yards peppered with exotic coral-colored plants. This gloomy back area of Los Angeles was more of what I was accustomed to seeing in the South Bronx.

The cab driver dropped us off at a local shelter. A female attendant with a soft, welcoming smile greeted us. "Can I help you, ma'am?" the kind woman asked. Our mother explained that we were from the Bronx, New York, and had nowhere to stay. The woman welcomed us to stay at the shelter for as long as we needed. The shelter was the polar opposite of Martinique's brightly lit, well-furnished, art deco home where we'd stayed for over a week. It was as if we were on a different planet. The shelter's flickering fluorescent lights made the corridors and rooms eerily dim. The walls were a dingy beige color streaked with stains from leaky pipes. The gray-colored ceiling, from which loose plaster dangled, was like a dark cloud hovering overhead. Grimy couches with shredded backs and sunken cushions were used to furnish certain rooms.

The smiling angelic faces we'd seen when we first arrived in Los Angeles turned into furrowed brows and burdened expressions on the faces of the men, women, and children residing in the shelter. They all seemed unhappy. I could almost feel the weight of their depression on my small shoulders as we walked through the corridors. Some smelled as if they hadn't showered in weeks. Others appeared to have dime-size welts along their arms and legs from bedbugs. Little girls held dolls with no heads or arms, and little boys played with sharp-edged broken toy trucks and cars.

We passed a man sitting in the corridor having a conversation with an imaginary person sitting next to him. The man's clothes were ripped as if they had been slashed with a razor blade. Sections of his long un-kempt hair seemed to be clumps held together by mud. He seemed too weak and tired to swat the small army of flies that buzzed around his head. Other men and women were mentally ill, drunk, or drug addicts. There were runaway boys and girls who seemed to be about Colette's age. With no parental protection, these runaways were at the mercy of human predators who lurked in the dark corners of the shelter. Our mother looked upon these teenagers with great compassion. "I bet their parents are looking for them. That's somebody's child. Somebody's baby."

• • •

Like a warden welcoming inmates to prison, the shelter attendant showed us our cots and handed us three dingy towels and a bar of soap that had strands of hair clinging to it. Our mother graciously thanked the attendant for the soap and towels. As soon as the well-intentioned attendant walked away, our mother pulled out of the older suitcase a bar of white-label soap she kept in a dish and a few face towels she had packed. "We are going to use these instead," she told us as she handed us each a clean face towel.

We helped our mother drag our suitcases toward the women's bathroom. She grabbed my hand to take me in with her and Colette.

"Ma, I can't go in there! That's the girl's bathroom," I protested.

"You have to come with us, Googie. I'm not going to let you go into that other bathroom by yourself. It's probably not clean, and it may not be safe."

As soon as my mother opened the squeaky bathroom door, we were greeted by a pungent smell. We all covered our noses. The women's bathroom was filthy, infested with flies, and looked as if it hadn't been cleaned in months. There were rust rings around the sinks, and most of the mirrors were shattered or missing entirely. Beyond the rusted sinks were toilets in stalls without doors. The toilets, like the sinks, had rust rings along the inside of the bowl. Some had cracked seat covers, and others had no seat covers at all. "Do not touch or sit on those toilet seats! Squat over the toilet but do *not* sit down," our mother instructed us.

Beyond the toilet stalls was a communal shower that contained six rusty showerheads. During our stay at the shelter, we never used the showers. Our mother had us clean our bodies and brush our teeth at the sink while she policed the area. We and the other homeless residents of the shelter slept in an open area that was the size of a small school gym, where there were hundreds of cots lined up in an army-like arrangement. The mattresses we slept upon were thin, with holes and burn marks, as if recently salvaged from a home on fire. Instead of bedsprings, each mattress lay upon a metal frame that made it feel as if we were lying on the floor. Before getting into bed, our mother placed each of our shoes under a leg of each cot.

"Why are you putting our shoes under the bed legs, Ma?" I asked.

"To keep our shoes from getting stolen, Googie." She figured that a potential thief would have to lift the entire cot, with us on it, to pilfer our shoes. We couldn't afford any of our possessions to be stolen. Though we didn't have much, the little we did have was ours. She unpacked clothing for the following day and place it between the mattress and the hard metal cot to press out the wrinkles by morning. She also unpacked pants and jackets and bundled them to serve as pillows. She instructed us to sleep in our clothes because there were no blankets. She led us in a prayer for our safekeeping overnight.

Then she sat in a chair with her legs draped over our suitcases. She weighed about 200 pounds, and she thought the size of her legs would discourage anyone from attempting to steal our luggage. As she had done with Cecil Jr., Robert, and L'Tanya when they first arrived in New York City in 1954, our mother would sit in the nearby chair and watch over us as we slept.

• • •

For lunch and dinner, we went to a neighboring soup kitchen, where we'd get a bowl of soup comprised mostly of broth, and two slices of bread, a glass of water, and a peach. When I took a bite out of the peach, I noticed mushy brown patches in several areas. "I can't eat this peach, Ma. It's rotten."

She took a plastic butter knife and, with surgeon-like precision, cut off the rotten sections of the peach. When she was done, the once round peach was in the shape of a square with its pit partially exposed. "There you go, Googie. It's as good as new."

I looked at her incredulously. I questioned whether we were looking at the same peach. For breakfast the soup kitchen offered bananas, peaches, and apples, all of which were pocked with numerous brown spots as if they had leprosy. As she had done with the other peach, she cut off the rotten sections of the fruit. She'd also saved a few packs of Kellogg's Frosted Cherry Pop-Tarts to supplement our fruit-based breakfast.

Each morning, we helped our mother drag our luggage to the bathroom. Once we were done washing ourselves at the rusty sinks she would hand us toothbrushes and white-label toothpaste. "Brush your teeth, but do not lay your toothbrushes on the sink!"

• • •

In spite of our current situation, our mother had not forgotten about her promise to Colette to find Michael Jackson and the Jackson 5. During the fifth night of our stay at the shelter, our mother feverishly searched through her handbag. "Here it is!" She pulled out a small piece of paper that contained a name and telephone number.

"What is it, Ma?" Colette asked. Martinique had given her the telephone number of the photographer, Larry, who might know the address of the Jackson 5. She thought that he might have returned from his out of town assignment. She found a public phone, inserted a dime, and called him. Colette and I stood by her side with our bags as our mother waited for some one to answer. The phone seemed to ring endlessly. Finally a man's voice could be heard.

"Hello, Mr. Johnson. My name is Sodonia Luckie. Martinique gave me your number. She may have told you about us. My daughter Colette is a big fan of Michael Jackson and the Jackson 5, and we've traveled from New York City to California to find them. Can you help us? Do you know where they live?"

"Yes, Ms. Luckie, Martinque told me that I should expect your call. Unfortunately, I don't know where they live, but I know a colleague who may know the town and street they live on. Sorry, that's the best I can do."

"That's fine, we'll take whatever information you have."

"OK, Ms. Luckie, give me the telephone number where you are calling from, and I will call you back with the information."

"There is no telephone number on this phone. It's a public phone," my mother said.

"Where are you staying?" Mr. Johnson asked.

"Well, we are staying at a shelter in LA. We are just about out of money. We wanted to try to find them before we head back to the Bronx."

"You and your children are more than welcome to stay with us. I insist."

This was music to my mother's ears. "We'd really appreciate that, Mr. Johnson."

"OK, give me the address, and I'll come pick you up." Our mother quickly gave him the shelter's address.

"I'm on my way," he said before hanging up the phone.

Our mother grabbed our bags and led us to the front door of the shelter. She thanked the attendant for allowing us to stay. We waited on the curbside until Mr. Johnson arrived.

Like a knight in shining armor, a handsome African American man showed up in a station wagon. "Ms. Luckie?" he asked.

"Yes!" my mother replied.

"I'm Larry. Let me help you with your bags."

Our mother introduced us, and he chuckled after saying my name. Mr. Johnson opened the car door for my mother.

My mother turned to me and said, "See, Googie. Chivalry is not dead." Within minutes of meeting him, Mr. Johnson taught me that women like having doors opened for them. Our mother sat in the front with Mr. Johnson and Colette and I sat in the back. As the car pulled away from the curb, I looked out the back window at the shelter we were leaving behind. After nearly a week at the shelter, I had a greater appreciation of our small apartment at 738 Metcalf Avenue in the South Bronx.

HAYVENHURST

An hour after leaving the shelter, we arrived in a middle-class neighborhood in the San Fernando region of Los Angeles called Sherman Oaks. We pulled into the driveway. Unlike the Clason Point apartments, a two-car garage separated each home in Sherman Oaks. Mr. Johnson's three-bedroom home was modestly spacious. The grass in the front yard was cut with such evenness it lay like a lush carpet. The well-manicured yard complemented the deep red rosebushes planted beneath the living-room window and tall palm tree that stood curbside. As Mr. Johnson unloaded our luggage, Mrs. Johnson and their daughter greeted us. "Hey, honey, this is Ms. Luckie and her children, Colette and Googie."

"Hello," Mrs. Johnson said. She was a soft-spoken woman who reminded me of Julia, a character played by Diahann Carroll in a 1970 show of the same name. Given how attractive Mrs. Johnson and Martinique were, I was convinced that beauty was a prerequisite for women living in Los Angeles.

"This is my daughter, Cheryl," Mr. Johnson said.

Cheryl, who was about Colette's age, was fair-skinned with long sandy-brown hair. At the time of the introduction, Colette had a *Right On!* magazine in her hand that had a picture of the Jackson 5 on the cover.

"Do you like the Jackson 5, too?" Cheryl asked Colette.

"Yes! I love them. Especially Michael!"

Colette and Cheryl hit it off immediately. She took Colette to her room. Cheryl could have easily fit in with Colette's fellow Jackson 5-loving friends in the Bronx.

"Thank you for allowing us to stay at your home," our mother said graciously to the Johnsons.

"No problem at all. You can stay as long as you like." Following nearly a week of living at the shelter, this home was like heaven on earth.

"So, Martinique tells me you may have an idea as to where the Jackson 5 live," our mother said.

"I don't have their address. But a colleague told me he heard they live in Encino, a town not too far from Sherman Oaks, on a street called Hayvenhurst. Unfortunately, it is a pretty long street. The Jackson home could be anywhere."

Undeterred by Mr. Johnson's comment regarding the length of Hayvenhurst, she said, "We will search for their home tomorrow." Our mother had not come this far to give up now. She was prepared to knock on every door along Hayvenhurst until a member of the Jackson family answered one.

The next afternoon, our mother told Colette and me to get dressed. "Where are we going, Ma?" Colette asked.

"We're going to try to find the Jacksons today."

Colette was eager to begin the search for Michael Jackson and the Jackson 5. She began to unroll the large pink curlers. Unfortunately, Colette's curls did not hold, so our mother used the pick to style Colette's hair in an Afro. When she was done, Colette's Afro was the size of a beach ball.

We had just enough money to take a cab to Encino.

"Where to, ma'am?" the cab driver asked.

"Encino."

"Where in Encino, ma'am?"

"Hayvenhurst Avenue," she said.

"Do you have an address, ma'am?"

"No, sir, just drop us off on a major street intersecting with Hayvenhurst."

The cab driver drove us to Encino. Approximately fifteen minutes later, he informed our mother, "We are approaching Hayvenhurst, ma'am. But it's a long street."

"Well, drop us off on the busiest cross street."

"That would be Ventura Boulevard, ma'am."

"That's fine. We'll walk from there." From the expression in his eyes, which we could see in his rearview mirror, the cab driver was perplexed by my mother's request. He let us out on the corner of Ventura Boulevard and Hayvenhurst.

We stood on the corner waiting for our mother to decide which direction to take. "Which way should we go, Ma, right or left?"

Our mother had no idea which direction to choose. She looked both ways down Hayvenhurst as far as her eyes could see. "Let's go right."

We couldn't believe our eyes as we walked down the street. There were several homes on Hayvenhurst that resembled the mansion I'd seen on a popular comedy show called *The Beverly Hillbillies*. Each mansion had curbside gates that were approximately six feet high. Each driveway seemed to go for miles, winding from the gate to the mansion's front door. Most gates were equipped with an intercom because of the distance to the front door of the mansion. We started walking down the long block.

One by one, our mother rang the bells on each intercom. The first two intercoms did not produce an answer from the residents. Colette became sadder with each unanswered bell.

We approached the next mansion. Our mother rang the bell on the intercom. "Yes, may we help you?" a voice asked.

"Yes, we are the Luckie family from the Bronx, New York. Do the Jacksons live here?" our mother asked.

"No, ma'am. Sorry."

We searched for hours. We kept walking, trying myriad intercoms on each side of the street. By the time we arrived at the tenth home, Colette began to look dejected.

"Colette," our mother said, noticing the sad expression on her daughter's face, "we've come too far to give up now. If I have to ring every intercom on Hayvenhurst, I will do it. We will find them!" Our mother's confidence and determination resurrected Colette's spirit.

"OK, Ma," Colette said as she wiped the tears that began to well in her eyes."

"Hey, there is a man in his yard, let's go ask him," our mother said as she pointed to a man a few mansions down the block. He was a chubby gentleman with silver hair. He was mowing the huge front lawn. We walked close to the gate. Our mother waved to capture the man's attention over the roaring lawn mower. The man cut off his mower and approached us. "Can I help you?"

"Yes, we are the Luckies from the Bronx. My daughter loves Michael Jackson and the Jackson 5. Do you know where they live?"

The man was quiet for a moment. "I can't tell you exactly where they live," he said.

"Thanks anyway," our mother said. We all turned to continue our search. As we walked away, we heard the man say, "But..."

We gave him our undivided attention.

"You're close. Real close. You're heading in the right direction." He nodded his head in the direction of a neighboring mansion, smiled at us, and winked.

"Thank you, sir," our mother said quietly to the kind gentleman. "By the way, you have a lovely home."

"This isn't my home. I work here. I'm the grounds keeper."

I couldn't believe it. There were people who were wealthy enough to afford landscapers, butlers, and maids. I thought such arrangements only existed on TV shows.

Our mother held our hands as we crossed the street and headed for the gate that the silver-haired man nodded toward. The property dwarfed all those we had visited before. Beautiful green plants and trees served as natural camouflage for the estate. At the entry was a white gate that appeared to be approximately ten feet tall. It had solid white trim and white bars that ran vertically along its front. Beyond the gate was a long driveway, at the end of which several cars were parked. Above the left side of the tall gate, nestled among the trees, was a small closed-circuit security camera. To the left of the gate, below the camera, was an intercom.

Our mother approached the intercom, pushed the button, and awaited a response as she had done with the other mansions we visited on Hayvenhurst.

"Yes, may we help you?" a voice asked.

"We are the Luckie family from the Bronx, New York. We took a Greyhound bus from New York City to California to find and meet the Jackson 5. My daughter Colette is a big fan. We don't want to come into your home. We just want to know if the Jackson 5 live here. Can you tell us?"

There was absolute silence. We waited what seemed to be hours for a response. Our mother stared at the intercom and then looked at Colette, whose eyes had begun to well with tears.

"Don't cry, Colette," I said. "We'll find Michael." Some of my mother's faith had rubbed off on me.

"Yes. Listen to your little brother," my mother suggested. With no response from the mysterious voice that had greeted us over the intercom, it seemed we'd have to continue our search. We turned to leave the front gate entrance and began to walk toward a neighboring home in search of Michael Jackson and the Jackson 5.

Suddenly, a voice over the intercom said, "Come in." The huge white gate slowly opened. As we looked down the driveway, a tomato-red 450 Mercedes Benz sports car was approaching. We were in a state of shock and didn't know what to expect. As the car pulled up next to us, the driver rolled down the window. We could not believe our eyes as we looked into the luxurious car. It was Jermaine Jackson. "Hello, my name is Jermaine."

He did not have to introduce himself to us. We knew who he was.

I thought, *Wow, he looks just like the J5 cartoon character!*

Colette began to weep.

"Don't cry," he said softly to Colette as she wept uncontrollably. "My mother will meet you all at the end of the driveway," he said graciously as he pointed down the driveway. He flashed the patented Jackson smile and drove off.

Halfway down the driveway, we could see the silhouette of a woman. Like characters from *The Wizard of Oz*, we walked through the open gate and down the long driveway. On the left side of the driveway was a well-manicured lawn with beautiful trees and lush colorful plants. On the right side, a line of equally beautiful trees that seemed to stand at attention. Nailed onto one of the trees was a yellow street sign with black lettering that read JACKSON 5 BLVD.

Honorary Jackson 5 BLVD. street sign at Hayvenhurst Estate. California 1973.

We could see Mrs. Jackson's angelic face as she patiently waited for us. "Hello, welcome to our home." Like Jermaine, Mrs. Jackson was soft-spoken, gracious, and kind. She wore an Afro and a white jacket draped over her shoulders with a multicolored blouse beneath. Mrs. Jackson reached out her hand to shake our mother's hand.

"Thank you for allowing us into your home, Mrs. Jackson," our mother said.

"I heard your story, Ms. Luckie. You came all the way from New York on a Greyhound bus to meet our family?"

"Yes, Mrs. Jackson. My daughter Colette is a big fan."

Colette was speechless and still had tears in her eyes.

"Say hello, Colette," our mother said as if to snap Colette out of a trance.

"Hello, Mrs. Jackson."

"Hello, Colette. And is this your youngest?"

"Yes. This is my son, Googie."

"Googie?" Mrs. Jackson responded incredulously with a slight chuckle. "Hello, Googie." When she smiled, she looked like her sons.

"Hi!" I waved at Mrs. Jackson as if she were standing a mile away.

"Come on in. I'll show you around and introduce you to the rest of our family."

"Thank you, Mrs. Jackson. By the way, would you mind taking a picture with Colette?"

"Of course not," Mrs. Jackson said.

Colette, sporting her beach ball-size Afro and dressed in white hot pants and a bright red blouse with a glittery question mark, posed for a picture with the mother of her idols.

Mrs. Jackson with Colette at Hayvenhurst Estate. California 1973.

Walking with a slight limp,[26] Mrs. Jackson escorted us into the Jackson estate. We were amazed that this mother of arguably the five most famous brothers in the world was so welcoming and gentle. "Are you originally from New York?"

"My children were born and raised in the Bronx, New York. I was born in the Midwest—Junction City, Kansas."

"Our family lived in Gary, Indiana, before moving here."

"Yes, we know," our mother said with a big smile. Colette had taught my mother and me everything there was to know about the Jackson

---

26 Mrs. Jackson contracted polio at two years old. The disease left her with a permanent limp. https://en.wikipedia.org/wiki/Katherine_Jackson (October 7, 2013).

family, including where they lived before moving to Encino and becoming superstars.

Mrs. Jackson continued to speak with us and ask us questions as if we were longtime neighbors.

As we walked toward the house, we saw several cars parked at the end of the driveway. A luxurious green car with a white interior and a white top captured my attention. I saw Jackie about to enter the car. "Ma, there's Jackie!"

Mrs. Jackson heard my comment and asked Jackie to wait a moment before leaving. Jackie, who normally performed in dazzling outfits on stage, wore a striped shirt and denim overalls. He paused to hear his mother's request.

Mrs. Jackson escorted us to the car and introduced us to her eldest famous son. "Jackie, these are the Luckies from the Bronx, New York."

"Hello. How are you?" Jackie asked in a soft high-pitched voice. He seemed to be in a bit of a rush and had a friend waiting for him seated in the passenger seat. He got in the car and started the engine.

Before he pulled out of the driveway, our mother asked him, "Would you mind taking a picture with my daughter?"

"Not at all," Jackie responded. Without getting out of the car, Jackie leaned toward his open window. Colette leaned on the car for the photo op. Our mother took the picture with her Kodak camera. Jackie smiled, waved at us, and drove out of the driveway.

Jackie Jackson with Colette at Hayvenhurst Estate. California 1973.

We passed a basketball hoop with a rim that was hung with a pristine white net. "Ma, the Jackson 5 play basketball too?" I innocently asked. I was amazed that these guys liked to play basketball.

Shortly after Jackie drove away, Marlon came out of the house to greet us. Though he was polite enough to introduce himself, an introduction from the superstar was unnecessary. "Hello, my name is Marlon."

"Nice to meet you, Marlon," my mother responded.

Colette was speechless and simply waved.

I spoke up. "Hi, Marlon!"

We had watched him on TV gracefully dance between Jackie and Tito as he sang with his world famous brothers. We had grown accustomed to seeing him in brilliant outfits during performances, but he was dressed casually like his brother, Jackie. He wore white slacks, a yellow shirt with the J5 heart logo, and a tan summer hat with a colorful hatband.

Marlon was hospitable and congenial. He seemed to have genuine interest in us. "When did you arrive in Los Angeles? How long are you staying? How long did it take you to get here on the bus?" Marlon was completely engaged in the conversation and listened intently to our answers. Marlon was the kind of polite, well-mannered teenage boy that my mother hoped Colette would bring home when she started to date.

"Well, nice meeting you all," Marlon said as he started to go back inside. Before you go, Marlon, would you mind taking a picture with Colette and Googie?"

Marlon posed with us. Marlon stood on Colette's left side, and I—dressed in white slacks, red shirt, and multicolored jacket—stood on Colette's right side with my outstretched arm barely reaching her shoulder. We all smiled as our mother took our picture.

Marlon Jackson with Colette and me at Hayvenhurst Estate. California 1973.

"Nice meeting you, Marlon," our mother said.

"Nice meeting all of you, too," Marlon said.

"Well, he was really nice...and cute, too," my mother whispered to Colette. After meeting Marlon, our mother was convinced he was the one for her daughter.

But Colette had her heart set on another Jackson—Michael.

Mrs. Jackson took us through a sliding glass door into the house. I couldn't believe my eyes. The family room was huge.

"Please come and have a seat," Mrs. Jackson kindly said. There were two or three small stairs that led down to a sunken area with the plushest furniture I'd ever seen. The sofas were soft and almost seemed to caress us as we sat down.

"Hey, Ma, their couch doesn't have any plastic on it," I said, referring to the uncomfortable plastic that covered our small sofa at our Clason Point apartment. Mrs. Jackson smiled at my remark as if she'd knew what I was referring to.

"You have a beautiful home, Mrs. Jackson," our mother said as she looked around the area.

"Thank you," Mrs. Jackson humbly replied.

Beyond the family room was an open kitchen area with appliances that I'd only seen awarded to contestants on *Let's Make a Deal*. I noticed a bowl of colorful fruit on the kitchen counter. It appeared far fresher than the fruit offered by the shelter. "Mrs. Jackson, can I have some fruit?" I boldly asked. I hadn't had anything to eat since our search began on Hayvenhurst.

"Googie!" my mother reprimanded me.

"That's OK, Ms. Luckie," Mrs. Jackson said to assuage my mother's feeling of embarrassment. "You can have some fruit, Googie."

I believe Mrs. Jackson found me somewhat amusing. Given the size of my Afro, I may have reminded her of one of her own sons at a younger age. I ran to the kitchen area and grabbed a couple of pieces of fruit from the bowl. The fruit looked nothing like the fruit we purchased at the local stores in the Bronx or were offered at the Los Angeles shelter. The grapes, plums, nectarines, and apples were rich hues of purple, red, and green. There wasn't a rotten piece of fruit in the bowl.

After I got my fruit, Mrs. Jackson gave us a tour of their beautiful estate. She led us from the living room back out the sliding glass doors. The backyard covered approximately two acres. The grass was exceptionally thick and deep green. Beautiful trees and exotic plants surrounded the area, providing the Jackson family with a natural source of privacy. I felt as if I were in the Garden of Eden.

There was a big swimming pool with crystal-clear water, and a white slide that led into the water. I imagined myself climbing to the top and coming down the slide with my arms fully extended, splashing into the pristine water below. Mrs. Jackson walked us around the pool area to a small yellow house. "This is the game room."

The Jackson 5 had a game room with the latest pinball machines. The entire room was lit up like a Christmas tree. Just beyond the game room was a recording studio. "And this is where they rehearse." We looked through the window and saw instruments, microphones on stands, and myriad recording equipment.

Colette recalled Jermaine disclosing during his interview on WWRL that he'd recorded a promotion for the July 22 "Skywriter" concert in New York in the Jackson's personal recording studio[27]. She'd never imagined that one day she'd be standing just outside the studio where that recording was made. As our mother stared at the recording studio where the famous group rehearsed, she leaned over and whispered to Colette, "I wish I had brought my Super 8 camera."

We circled the rest of the property and headed back toward the sliding doors we'd entered. As we entered the home and returned to the living-room area, other members of the Jackson family greeted us. "Ms. Luckie, Colette, Googie, this is my daughter La Toya."

La Toya was an attractive young girl who appeared to be about Colette's age. I was mesmerized. Her beauty confirmed my belief that being pleasing to the eyes was a qualification for women to become residents of California. As I stared at her beautiful face, I noticed some resemblance to Michael. With the unfiltered honesty of an eight-year-old boy, I pointed and said, "She has a nose like Michael!" La Toya laughed and covered up her nose with both hands. She and a few of her teenage girlfriends then left the home. From their discussion, they seemed to be preparing to go shopping.

Our mother leaned over to Colette and whispered, "Do you want to go with them? I can ask Mrs. Jackson, if you like."

But Colette did not come all the way from the Bronx to go shopping. She came to see Michael, and she wouldn't let a day of shopping with other teenage girls get in the way of that. "No, Ma," Colette whispered back, "I'd rather see Michael."

Mrs. Jackson then introduced us to the youngest member of the family "And this is my youngest daughter, Janet."

"Hi!" Janet said with the patented Jackson smile. Janet and I were about the same age. We seemed to hit it off instantly. She was personable

---

27 Gordon Skene, "Newstalgia Pop Chronicles, An Interview With The Jackson 5, 1973," http://newstalgia.crooksandliars.com/gordonskene/interview-jackson-5-1973#sthash.B7eLQQNk.FiQVXXyf.dpbs (June 25, 2012).

and friendly. I imagined the size of my Afro made her feel as if she were hanging out with a younger version of one of her brothers.

"Janet, why don't you take Googie over there and watch TV."

I followed Janet to an area not too far from the sunken living room. The TV screen was tall and wide. In comparison to our old second-hand, floor-model television, theirs seemed as big as that used at our neighborhood Whitestone Drive-In. Janet, like most kids our age, liked cartoons. She turned to a channel that showed Disney cartoons. Mickey, Pluto, Donald, Goofy, and the other Disney characters mesmerized me as they moved across the humongous screen. The TV screen made the Disney characters seem as tall as Janet and me. I was spellbound by the vibrant shades of red, blue, yellow, and other colors. Up to this point, I'd only seen Mickey and his faithful companions in black and white.

As she laughed at the characters on the humongous screen, I said, "You look just like Michael." She displayed the patented Jackson smile after hearing my remark. Little did I know, at the time, that several years later the little girl who sat by my side watching Mickey Mouse would be cast as Penny Gordon Woods on the comedy hit TV show, *Good Times*.[28] We'd met every member of the Jackson 5, except two. Tito, who had gotten married, was not at the Jackson estate. The other Jackson we hadn't met was Michael.

Mrs. Jackson and our mother spent a few minutes conversing as if they were old friends. Colette politely leaned over to our mother and whispered in her ear, "Where's Michael?"

Our mother, who was sitting next to Mrs. Jackson on the plush sofa said, "We appreciate you allowing us into your lovely home and introducing us to your beautiful children. But my daughter loves Michael and was wondering if he was around." As soon as our mother finished her sentence, someone in a red union suit ran across the room.

Colette noticed the figure. Excited by the unexpected appearance of her teen idol and unable to find the proper wording, she erroneously screamed out, "There it goes! There it goes!" It was Michael Jackson.

---

28 "Janet Jackson," http://en.wikipedia.org/wiki/Janet_Jackson#1966.
   E2.80.9382:_Childhood_and_television_work (November 4, 2013).

"Michael, Michael!" Mrs. Jackson apologized. "I'm so sorry, Ms. Luckie, Michael is truly shy. Excuse me."

Mrs. Jackson followed Michael. Approximately five minutes later, she returned without him. "I'm so sorry, Michael is so shy…and he is a little embarrassed that his hair isn't quite combed."

I was amazed by her comments. *How could he be shy?* I thought. *Was this the same Michael who appeared on the Flip Wilson Show? Was this the same Michael who had dazzled millions of teenage girls, including my own sister, as he sang and danced on stage? How could someone who was so bold on stage, be so shy off it?*

Shortly thereafter, Mr. Jackson walked into the living room. Mrs. Jackson introduced us to Mr. Jackson. My mother shook Mr. Jackson's hand, as did Colette and I.

"Colette would love to meet Michael, but he won't come out," Mrs. Jackson repeated. Mr. Jackson walked in the direction where Michael had run. A few moments later, there he was. Michael Jackson. He wore a black wide-brimmed hat. It covered up most of his Afro, though a good portion of it seemed to flow out of the bottom of the hat. He sat quietly next to his mother. "Michael, these are the Luckies from New York."

"Hello. Nice to meet you," a soft-spoken Michael said. That was followed by the boyish smile we had seen in images plastered on Colette's bedroom walls and on the *Got to Be There* album cover Colette kissed before she went to sleep. Here was Colette's teen idol sitting right in front of us.

In spite of the odds, our mother had accomplished her mission. Her daughter was finally sitting within arm's length of Michael Jackson. We all sat there, eerily silent. Our mother and Mrs. Jackson looked at Colette waiting for her to say something to Michael or ask him a question. However, Colette was completely star struck.

Our mother finally broke the uncomfortable silence. "Well, Colette, here he is. Michael Jackson," she said with an incredible sense of accomplishment. "Aren't you going to say anything to him?"

Colette was speechless.

Then my mother asked the unthinkable: "Aren't you going to kiss him?"

Colette looked completely shocked, as if her deepest secrets had been revealed. Mrs. Jackson smiled at the look on Colette's face. Colette uttered no words, but she smiled nervously.

"Well," our mother continued, "If you won't, I will." In motherly fashion, our mother reached over and gave Michael a kiss on his cheek and softly stroked the side of his face. Michael looked from underneath the brim of his hat and smiled. As soon as our mother and Mrs. Jackson resumed their conversation, Michael was gone. It was as if he had vanished.

As the night approached, and stars began to fill the sky, we prepared to leave. We had had an unbelievable day, spending time with the Jackson family at their lovely home. In spite of their fame and fortune, the Jacksons were humble and gracious. My mother thanked Mrs. Jackson endlessly for her hospitality. Mrs. Jackson walked us out of the sliding doors and toward the driveway. She briefly turned back in her home to retrieve the white jacket she was wearing when we first met her at the driveway. While Mrs. Jackson was in her home, our mother asked Colette to take a picture of her in the back of the Jackson estate. Colette quickly snapped a picture of our mother.

My mother, Sodonia Luckie, at Jacksons' Hayvenhurst Estate. California 1973.

Mrs. Jackson returned with her white jacket over her shoulders and escorted us down the driveway. "How long are you going to be in California?" she asked my mother.

"Probably for a few more days. Then we will be heading back home to the Bronx." My mother did not mention that we had to leave because we had just about run out of money and food stamps.

What Mrs. Jackson said next nearly knocked us off our feet. "We are having a thank-you party on September 9th and would like to have you, Colette, and Googie as our guests. Do you think you can make it? Can you come back?"

Colette and I looked at each other with expressions of shock. Our mother smiled at Colette and asked, "Would you like that, Colette? Do you want to come back for the party?"

A speechless Colette nodded yes. Tears began to well up in her eyes again. "Of course, thank you so much."

Mrs. Jackson said, "So we'll see you back here in a few days."

"Yes, and thanks again," our mother said. She and Mrs. Jackson embraced as if they'd been friends for years. We continued down the long driveway past the tree with the JACKSON 5 BLVD sign. As we approached the white gate, we could hear that familiar rumbling sound. The white gate opened as we walked toward it. We turned around to see Mrs. Jackson's silhouette in the distance, waving good-bye. The huge gate then shut behind us.

Me at entrance of Jacksons' Hayvenhurst Estate. California 1973.

Colette and I couldn't believe what just happened. Our mother's ability to look beyond the impossible resulted in her not only fulfilling her promise to her daughter of meeting Michael Jackson and members of the Jackson 5, but also returning to the Hayvenhurst estate for a party hosted by the Jackson family. Our mother, on the other hand, never lost faith that we would meet the Jackson 5. "I told you we would find them. Didn't I?" our mother said with a confident grin. "Well, we did it! You got to meet Michael Jackson and his family."

Colette had tears in her eyes. She was overwhelmed by the entire experience. Too emotional to speak.

"Yes, Ma, and Janet and I watched Mickey Mouse. Did you see how big and colorful he was on their TV?"

My mother and Colette smiled at me, acknowledging that what most impressed an eight-year-old boy was hanging out with a kid my age and watching cartoons.

As we walked away from the Jackson estate, Colette let out a high-pitched scream. "We met Michael! We met the Jackson 5!" Given the intensity of this outburst, it appeared she'd been holding in this emotion during our entire visit at the Jackson's Hayvenhurst estate. "Thank you, Ma, for making this dream come true," Colette said. She hugged our mother as if she'd never let go. "I can't believe you kissed Michael!"

"Yes, girl. I did."

"How was it, Ma? How did Michael's face feel?" Colette asked and waited with bated breath for our mother to answer.

"Colette, Michael's face was really soft. Kissing his cheek was like kissing a beautiful, soft, chocolate cloud. When I rubbed the side of his cheek with my hand, it was so soft."

As our mother shared an experience that Colette and millions of other teenage girls only dreamed of, Colette stood with her hands clasped over her mouth to mute her scream. "I still can't believe you did that."

"Why didn't you kiss him when I asked, Colette? Don't you always kiss his album cover before you go to bed?"

Colette smiled sheepishly.

"And we are coming back to their home in a few days," our mother exclaimed. "I'll have my Super 8 camera with me when we return for the party."

Our mother's ability to believe in the impossible, and the love for her daughter, had taken us almost three thousand miles from packing our bags at 738 Metcalf Avenue to sitting on a couch with Michael Jackson at the Jackson Hayvenhurst estate. Her faith had driven her to save food stamps and welfare checks to get us across the country, forfeit two months' rent, and reside at a Los Angeles shelter for almost a week so that her daughter could live her dream.

During our walk toward Ventura Blvd, we reminisced about our visit with the Jacksons. Our mother spoke about the graciousness of the Jackson family.

Colette asked, "Ma, why do you think Mrs. Jackson let us in their house?"

Our mother paused to consider her daughter's thought-provoking question. "Well, Mrs. Jackson is a mother also. As a mother, there is nothing I wouldn't do for you or any of my children. I imagine there is nothing that Mrs. Jackson wouldn't do for her daughters or sons. There is nothing like a mother's love for her children." She continued, "And after Mrs. Jackson heard how we took a Greyhound bus from New York to California, she may have been reminded of their humble beginnings in Gary, Indiana."

On the corner of Ventura and Hayvenhurst, where the cab driver had dropped us off earlier that day, our mother began to sing an old Frank Sinatra classic. "Fairy tales can come true, it can happen to you..." She continued to hum the melody as we hailed a cab.

When we arrived back at the Johnson home, Mr. Johnson greeted us at the door. "Well, how did it go?"

"We found them and spent most of the day at their home!" our mother said.

"Congratulations!" Mr. Johnson said. "Your persistence paid off."

My mother didn't know how to tell the Johnsons that we'd gotten invited back for a party. She didn't want them to feel bad. However, since the Johnsons had been kind enough to allow us to stay at their home, she decided to reveal the unexpected benefit of our visit with the Jacksons. "Mrs. Jackson invited us back for a private party in a few days." Our mother paused to see Mr. Johnson's response.

"That's wonderful!" Mr. Johnson said with genuine excitement.

"Thank you, Mr. Johnson. I wish we could bring your family along."

"Oh, Ms. Luckie. Don't you worry about that," Mr. Johnson replied.

"We couldn't have done it without you, Mr. Johnson. Looking for the Jackson 5 in California would have been like looking for a needle in a haystack without the information you provided."

Mrs. Johnson said, "You brought your children all the way from the Bronx to find the Jackson 5. You deserve to be at the party. Enjoy it and please tell us all about it."

"Is it OK for Colette to share the news with your daughter? Or should she not mention it?" our mother asked Mr. and Mrs. Johnson.

"Of course Colette should let Cheryl know. She'll be excited for her," Mrs. Johnson responded.

Moments after Colette walked into Cheryl's room to greet her, there was a sudden scream. We heard Cheryl say, "Colette, you have to tell me all about it!"

This lovely family was genuinely excited that our trip from New York was not in vain. They, like the Jacksons, were also gracious. This would be a day that we would never forget. With the Jackson 5 thank-you party about three days away, the best was yet to come.

THANK-YOU PARTY

On the afternoon of September 9, a few days after our initial visit to the Jackson estate, we took a cab from the Johnsons' home to attend the Jacksons' thank-you party. This event was in appreciation of all those who had contributed to the success of the Jackson 5.

"Where to, ma'am?" the cab driver asked.

"Encino, 4641 Hayvenhurst, please." It was another beautiful sunny day in Southern California, where it seemed to never rain. The sky was as blue as the Pacific Ocean. The warm breeze caressed my face as I leaned my head toward the open cab window. As the cab turned onto Hayvenhurst, we passed the mansion where the silver-haired grounds keeper had given us a hint as to where the Jacksons lived. The cab dropped us off in front of the large white gate at the entryway of the Jackson estate.

Once again my mother spoke into the intercom, but this time it was without trepidation.

"May we help you?"

"Yes. We are the Luckie family. We were invited to the thank-you party by Mrs. Jackson."

The gate rumbled as it opened. Colette turned to our mother and said, "I can't believe we are here…again!" Our mother unpacked her Super 8 camera and began to film as we walked down the long driveway. We passed the red Benz roadster Jermaine was driving when he invited us into his home on our first visit. As we drew closer to the house, we heard

119

laughter and R&B music. There seemed to be hundreds of people at the party, a multiethnic sea of smiling faces.

Marlon Jackson noticed us in the crowd and greeted us. "Welcome back! Glad you could make it!"

We were amazed that this superstar remembered us. He greeted and treated us as if he'd known us for years. Marlon wore a checkered white shirt with blue lines and matching blue pants. His medium-size Afro was perfectly round. He escorted us to his mother, who was standing in a crowd of guests. Mrs. Jackson greeted us with her angelic smile. She wore a conservative red-and-white-checkered short-sleeved suit with a white blouse. Mrs. Jackson's hair wasn't styled in the Afro like a few days before. It appeared more permed and fell just above her shoulders. The sun seemed to dance in her hair making her face seem even more angelic than a few days before. "Welcome back and thank you for coming to our party," Mrs. Jackson said to us. She and our mother embraced as if they were longtime friends.

"Thank you for having us, Mrs. Jackson," Colette said.

"Glad you could make it, Colette. Enjoy the party." Mrs. Jackson then began to greet many other guests. As we came to the end of the driveway, where several of the Jackson vehicles were parked, we saw several well-dressed guests in jump suits and platform shoes having a casual shoot-around with a red, white, and blue ABA basketball. There was another dapper young man shooting jump shots with the guests. It was Tito. He wore a plaid cream-colored shirt with a brown vest, brown pants, and cream-colored platform shoes. He also sported a cream wide-brimmed hat with a dark hatband. The portion of his Afro that couldn't be contained in the crown of his hat flowed from beneath its wide brim.

Tito Jackson on basketball court at Jacksons' thank-you party. Hayvenhurst Estate 1973.

"Tito looks sharp!" I said to my mother.

Many of the guests wore the latest fashions of the early seventies. The men wore bell-bottoms, shirts with long lapels, applejack hats, and platform shoes, with Afros of various sizes. Many of the women wore hot pants that flared at the bottom. Some wore two-piece pantsuits with wide-brimmed hats. Their tops ranged from lingerie-like blouses to fitted tube tops. The style of their hair varied. Some had perms that produced flowing smooth hair, and others wore Afros or "naturals." Colette and I also wore popular seventies fashions that allowed us to blend into the fashionably dressed crowd.

Colette wore a lavender two-piece hot-pants set. Her bikini top tied in a knot at the middle of her chest, exposing her smooth stomach. Though she was only thirteen, Colette had a shape of a woman twice her age. She would inherit the voluptuous shape of her mother and Flossie, her grandmother. Colette's outfit accentuated every curve of her maturing body. She also had a large round Afro. Colette's outfit and huge hair captured the attention of many guests at the party.

My mother dressed me in a burgundy jacket, white turtleneck shirt, and white-and-burgundy plaid bell-bottoms that looked as if they were cut from a picnic tablecloth. I wore burgundy platform shoes, and a burgundy-and-white striped belt, and my basketball-size Afro.

Our mother wore a pink dress that ended just below her knees. Her jet-black wavy hair proclaimed her Mexican heritage. Colette, our mother, and I walked around the pool area and mingled with the guests as music filled the air. Here we were, the Luckie family from the Bronx, attending the "hottest" party in California hosted by the most popular music family group in the world. I looked across the pool and saw Janet walking in the direction of the game room. "Hey, Ma, can I hang out with Janet over there?"

I pointed toward Janet. "OK, Googie, but don't run, and make sure you excuse yourself when walking through the crowd." In spite of my mother's instructions, I ran over to Janet, bumping into a few adults along the way. I arrived at the steps of the game room where Janet was standing. "Hi, Googie," Janet said in a soft-spoken tone similar to her brother Jermaine.

Janet wore white fitted bell-bottoms and a red-and-white off-the-shoulder blouse that had ruffles around the neckline. Her hair was set in a style that was popular among the girls in the Bronx. She had a small bun at the top of her head held together by a small barrette, and "baby hair," a style in which gel or Ultra Sheen conditioner was used to grease down a portion of the hair along the hairline to resemble that of a baby.

Janet Jackson and me at Jacksons' thank-you party. Hayvenhurst Estate 1973.

Janet and I spent most of the time walking around the pool observing the different guests at the party. Many were poolside, dancing. I felt as if I was watching an episode of *Soul Train*.

The party was superbly catered. There were several chefs, some of whom resembled Chef Boy-Ar-Dee, wearing white jackets and matching toques. The waiters wore pristine white jackets while serving beautifully arranged food and drinks from silver trays. The buffet tables were approximately ten feet long and decorated with beautiful green plants. On top of the tables were baskets containing impeccably arranged food. Delectable desserts were displayed, including ice cream, sundaes, and ice-cream sodas. In Clason Point, only our neighborhood Mr. Softee ice-cream truck offered such sweets. The melons, pineapples, grapes, and other fruits were amazingly fresh, as if picked the morning of the event.

Men and women of different ages and ethnicities dined together. African American men and women sat with women who looked like Jackie Onassis and Wall Street types wearing expensive suits. Janet and I sat at a table near the game room with a group of other kids.

Across the pool I saw Michael greeting guests with his boyish smile.

Michael Jackson greeting guest at Jacksons' thank-you party. Hayvenhurst Estate 1973.

As soon as a group of people started to build around Michael, he would politely excuse himself and disappear into the house. I remained amazed that this professional entertainer was a shy teenage boy offstage.

After Janet and I finished eating, she and I walked to the opposite side of the pool to observe the partying guests. We saw Eddie Kendricks from the Temptations and Junior Walker of the All-Stars. They, like the Jacksons, were Motown artists. I also saw a tall man with an Afro as big as my own. It was Don Cornelius, who hosted the hottest dance and music show, *Soul Train*. He said hello to Janet and reached down to shake my hand. His huge hand practically swallowed mine.

As Janet and I navigated our way through the mostly adult crowd, I saw a familiar and beautiful face. It was La Toya. She wore a burgundy-colored top with patterned bottom that included burgundy overtones meshed with white, along with a seventies-style cream conch-shaped hat. Curly locks flowed beautifully from beneath the hat and lay around her shoulders, encircling her angelic face.

Redd Foxx (forefront left) and La Toya Jackson (background right) at Jacksons' thank-you party. Hayvenhurst Estate 1973.

We crossed paths with her mother. "Are you both enjoying yourselves?"

"Yes!" we said almost in unison.

Mrs. Jackson posed for a picture with Redd Foxx and other guests.

Mrs. Jackson (second from right) and Redd Foxx (far right) at Jacksons' thank-you party. Hayvenhurst Estate 1973.

Among the paparazzi with their expensive camera equipment stood my mother, capturing every moment on her low-budget Super 8 camera. Janet and I continued to circle the pool. Standing near the sliding glass doors leading into the home stood Mr. Jackson and Jackie conversing with several guests. Mr. Jackson wore a multicolored jacket with a white shirt and white slacks. His Afro was as big as his famous sons'. Jackie wore a white warm-up jacket with dark slacks. Jackie's sunglasses made him look exceptionally cool and mysterious.

People also mingled on the driveway. Among them was Jermaine, who was smiling and fully engaged in a conversation. He wore brownish-dark slacks and a white warm-up jacket with blue trim around the collar and wrists, similar in style to the jacket his brother Jackie wore. He had the biggest Afro of all of the brothers. It was interesting to see the Jacksons dressed casually, after watching them in dazzling outfits on TV.

Jermaine Jackson at Jacksons' thank-you party. Hayvenhurst Estate 1973.

My mother discovered me mingling with the crowd in the driveway. "Go over and ask Jermaine to take a picture with you." She prepared her Super 8 camera.

Jermaine was standing near the basketball court. Jackie and several guests were playing a pick-up game. I ran toward Jermaine.

"Hi, nice to see you again!" Jermaine said to me in his soft voice.

"Hi, Jermaine, can you take a picture with me?" I pointed to my mother who was standing approximately five feet away aiming her camera in our direction.

"Sure."

I waved at the camera. Jermaine, in big-brother fashion, placed his hands on my shoulders and smiled at the camera. Given the size of our Afros, we appeared to be brothers. My mother disappeared into the burgeoning crowd after taking the pictures of Jermaine and me.

Jermaine Jackson and me at Jacksons' thank-you party. Hayvenhurst Estate 1973.

Though I had seen my mother, I hadn't seen Colette. I remained in the area and watched Jermaine's brothers play basketball with some of their friends and guests.

Then I went back toward the pool area. Over my shoulder, I saw a small figure catch up and walk alongside me. It was Janet. It was increasingly difficult for us to move about the party as the crowd grew.

A few of the guests on a grassy area on the side of the house played a game that resembled tennis. There was a net, but the rackets used were smaller than those used for tennis. They used a strange-looking ball that had feathers and seemed to float. "What are they playing over there?" I asked Janet.

"That's badminton," Janet replied in a soft voice.

"That's a weird ball they're playing with. Looks like they are whacking a bird back and forth."

Janet smiled. I never asked Janet if she wanted to play badminton, and she never offered. We continued to walk around the party, laughing at guests who were poor dancers. We made another stop at the beautifully arranged buffet table near the game room. I made a sandwich with two pieces of bread, fresh cold cuts, sliced cheese, and mayonnaise. I grabbed a soda and several pieces of lush fruit. Unlike the white-label cola brand I was accustomed to, Coke, Pepsi, Dr. Pepper, 7-Up, and other colorful canned brands were on display. Janet prepared her plate and grabbed a soda, and we sat at a nearby table to eat. I bit into the sandwich, and my mouth exploded with flavor. "What kind of meat is this?" I asked Janet.

"Ham" she replied.

After I tasted ham, it was always difficult for me to endure the taste (and aftertaste) of spiced ham. All of the fruit, food, and beverages offered at the Jackson party seemed to awaken my taste buds. I ate the best food I'd ever tasted, felt the summer zephyr on my skin, and watched myriad ethnicities converse, laugh, eat, and dance together. *Heaven must be like this*, I thought, which had first occurred to me several weeks before when we arrived in Los Angeles.

As we sat at the table, I saw Michael a few feet away. His dazzling smile caused him to stand out among the crowd. He seemed to glide along the poolside, effortlessly navigating through his guests as he shook their hands.

Michael Jackson mingles with guests at Jacksons' thank-you party. Hayvenhurst Estate 1973.

Michael, like his brothers, was dressed casually. He wore an untucked green-plaid shirt, green slacks that had gold-colored studs running down each leg, and dark platform shoes. Michael's Afro was perfectly shaped. As Michael walked away, a young woman reached out to touch his clothes with her fingertips. Once again, Michael disappeared.

Janet and I went into the game room, which was filled with flashing lights, sounds of pinball machines, and laughter.

"I don't have any quarters to play the games," I said.

"You don't need a quarter. It's free," Janet replied.

"What?" My mouth fell open. "Really?"

Janet laughed. She walked up to a game, push a bright red button and out popped a silver pinball ready for play. Playing some of the latest pinball machines at no charge was a dream come true for me—a dream that was a way of life for Janet, who stood and smiled as I played a few games.

We returned to the driveway, where people were watching Jackie, Marlon, and several guests playing basketball.

Randy, the youngest of the Jackson brothers, was there. A little older and taller than me, he was dressed in a casual plaid turtleneck shirt with rolled-up sleeves and matching burgundy slacks. Around his waist was a leather belt with imprints of the J5 heart logo and a J5 buckle. Randy had a cast on his right foot and used crutches to get around. Mrs. Jackson had explained to us that Randy had karate kicked an object and injured his foot. My mother, who was standing in the crowd of guests, took pictures of Randy and me. I waved at the camera with one hand and pointed at Randy's injured foot with the other. Needless to say, Randy did not appear happy that an eight-year-old kid was using his injury as a photo op. After my mother captured the picture, Randy simply hobbled away.

Randy Jackson at Jacksons' thank-you party. In background, Benz Roadster driven by Jermaine Jackson during our first visit to Hayvenhurst estate. 1973.

Tito and his wife, Delores "Dee Dee" Martes, were among the crowd of guest watching the pick-up basketball game. Delores, who like us was from New York, wore a black hat and a light-blue two-piece short-sleeved outfit with a black blouse. Like La Toya, Dolores's hair flowed onto her shoulders from underneath her hat. In Dolores's arms was their first child, Toriano Adaryll Jackson II.[29]

Once again, I saw Michael and his stunning smile as he greeted and spoke with guests gathered in the area. After speaking with guests and a few family members, Michael seemed to inconspicuously vanish.

---

29 "Tito Jackson," http://en.wikipedia.org/wiki/Tito_ Jackson#Personal_life, (March 6, 2014).

Michael Jackson speaking with guests at Jacksons' thank-you party. Hayvenhurst Estate 1973.

My mother emerged from the crowd and said to me, "Hey, Googie, look over there. It's Redd Foxx." I was familiar with Redd Foxx, who played Fred on *Sanford and Son*, a TV comedy about a father and son who owned a junkyard in the Watts section of Los Angeles. Our mother, Colette, and I watched the show regularly. We'd laugh hysterically when Fred, typically dressed in dirty overalls and a lumberjack shirt, referred to his well-mannered good-intentioned son, Lamont, as "you big dummy," attempted to avoid work by claiming he had arthritis while displaying a cramped hand, or pretended to have a heart attack to escape a problem situation by clutching his chest and saying, "It's the big one. I'm comin' to join you, Elizabeth," referring to his wife who'd already entered the "pearly gates."[30] We also enjoyed the confrontational exchanges between Fred and a no-nonsense African American woman named Aunt Esther, who often referred to Fred as a "fish-eyed, beady-eyed fool" or "a Brillo pad with eyes," and warned Fred and others by saying "Watch it, sucka!"[31] The Jackson 5 identified Redd Foxx as one of their favorite TV stars during the WWRL radio interview promoting their July 22 "Skywriter" concert in New York City. At the thank-you party, Redd Foxx was dressed nothing like his junkyard-owning alter ego, Fred. He wore a cream-colored leisure suit and a brown shirt with lapels

---

30   "Redd Foxx," http://en.wikipedia.org/wiki/Redd_Foxx#Marriages, (March 10, 2014).

31   "Quotes for Aunt Esther Anderson," http://www.imdb.com/character/ch0038727/quotes, (March 10, 2014).

that were so long they touched his shoulders. He also wore a matching applejack hat. He was with a woman who was elegantly dressed in a stunning white pantsuit that accentuated her beautiful chocolate-brown complexion. She wore a white hat with a brim that dipped in front of her forehead and eyes, making her look elegantly mysterious.

My mother, knowing how audacious I was, said to me, "Go over there and say hi to Redd Foxx."

As I approached him, he made a comment that had all of those standing near him laughing. Some were laughing so hard, tears streamed down their faces. Others laughed while bent over holding their stomachs as if they were in pain, begging him to stop. Finally, he took a step forward, almost stumbling over me. "Hello, Redd Foxx," I said as he looked down at me.

"Hey, it's li'l Rodney Allen Rippy!" Redd Foxx exclaimed to those standing nearby. He'd mistaken me for the then-famous little African American boy who appeared in countless Jack in the Box commercials.

"No, my name is Googie."

"Oh, Googie. You look like li'l Rippy," Redd Foxx replied as he gave me five. He mushed my hair with his hand. "Doesn't this kid look like Rodney Allen Rippy?" He asked those gathered around him. They nodded in agreement.

After I explained to Redd Foxx that my mother was filming us, he found where she was standing, playfully licked his lips, and tugged at the waistband of his pants.

● ● ●

Of all the famous and not-so-famous people I interacted with at the Jacksons' party, there was one person I rarely saw—Colette. In spite of kissing Michael's album cover at the beginning of each day and end of each night, she had suddenly become bashful. I noticed my mother and Colette in a secluded area on the side of the house near the badminton net. Colette was sitting on a low stone wall on the side of the house. My mother had a concerned expression on her face as she spoke with Colette. I wanted to find out what was going on. "I'll be right back, Janet," I said.

By this time, Janet had an entourage of kids who were touring the party with us. I ran to where Colette seemed to be hiding. Colette was so shy that she couldn't generate the courage to take a picture with Michael Jackson. She'd spent most of the time at the party quietly sitting near the badminton area.

My mother was pleading with Colette. "Colette, the sun is going down, and soon there will not be enough light for me to film you with Michael. Besides," she continued, "we came all the way from New York for you to meet Michael and take pictures with him. I'm starting to run out of film. If you don't let me film you with Michael, your friends will never forgive you. They may not even believe you met him."

Understanding that Colette was too shy to take a picture with her idol, I said, "Colette, why are you afraid to take a picture with Michael? He's just a human being."

As I tried to embolden my sister, Janet and her small entourage of kids approached us.

I had an idea. "Hey, Janet, would you mind taking a picture with my sister, Colette?" Janet nodded.

Colette finally got up off the small brick wall she was sitting on and allowed our mother to film her with Janet.

Janet Jackson with Colette at Jacksons' thank-you party. Hayvenhurst Estate 1973.

After the picture with Janet, I turned to Colette and said, "See, Colette. That wasn't so bad. Hey, look over there, it's Marlon. Let's go take a picture with him." Marlon was standing near the pool.

Colette finally began to walk toward Marlon. In motherly fashion, our mother asked "Marlon, would you mind taking a picture with Colette?"

Marlon posed with Colette, who waved at the camera as our mother continued to film. After my mother finished filming Colette with Marlon, I said, "That wasn't so bad either, was it?"

"No, Googie," Colette responded as she looked down and smiled at me.

"Now, let's go take a picture with Michael. I know where he is. I saw him sitting on a car in the driveway."

My mother smiled as I took Colette by her hand and led her to where I last saw Michael. After filming Colette with Janet and Marlon, our mother only had about three minutes of film remaining. The sun was setting. We were running out of light, film, and time. As we passed the house and the pool, we could hear cheering coming from the driveway. A crowd had formed a semicircle around the basketball court and was watching Tito and Jackie play a competitive game of basketball with friends and guests. Tito, who was dressed in slacks, dress shirt, and hat at the start of the party, now wore a gray sweat suit with white sneakers. Moments later, Marlon joined the game. He'd also changed from his casual outfit worn during the party to a dark warm-up suit with matching dark sneakers. Jackie had changed to a green sweat suit.

The Jackson brothers, in spite of their superstardom, were like most teenagers. As they played on the court, they looked no different from the guys who played pickup basketball at the big park in my neighborhood.

After the game, Tito took a break to spend time with Dee Dee, who was leaning against a car. Jermaine, who did not participate in the game, stood nearby. Suddenly, an attractive young woman I hadn't seen previously walked up to Jermaine and stood by his side. She had short hair with bangs and a beautiful brown complexion.

Jermaine Jackson (forefront left). Tito Jackson and Dolores "Dee Dee" Martes (background right) at Jacksons' thank-you party. Hayvenhurst Estate 1973.

Colette asked our mother, "Do you know who that girl is standing next to Jermaine?"

"No, Colette. She looks familiar. Who is she?" our mother asked. Colette, knowing all things pertaining to the Jackson 5, said, "That's Hazel Gordy, Berry Gordy's daughter."

"She sure looks like her dad," our mother said. Jermaine and Hazel would eventually marry.[32]

"There he is!" I pointed toward Michael. He was sitting on the back of Jackie's green car, rocking back and forth. Though family and friends surrounded him, Michael appeared to spend most of the time observing his brothers and listening to people talk.

---

32 "Jermaine Jackson," http://en.wikipedia.org/wiki/Jermaine_Jackson#Personal_life, (October 7, 2013).

Michael Jackson with guests at Jacksons' thank-you party. Hayvenhurst Estate 1973.

I took Colette by the hand. "Now remember, he's just a human being." Colette looked down at me, smiled, and tightly held my hand. I walked her over to Michael, who was smiling as we approached him. "See, Colette, look at him. He's just like us. He's a human being," I said to assuage Colette's shyness. To her, Michael was much more than that. As we walked toward Michael, Colette's grip on my hand continued to tighten. I asked, "Michael, would you take a picture with my sister Colette?"

"Sure," a soft-spoken Michael responded.

I led Colette to her idol. She stood next to Michael and waved at the camera. Michael still sat on the trunk of the car, leaning on his left arm. His right arm rested on his right leg. He smiled brilliantly as Colette stood beside him.

Mission accomplished. Colette was standing next to Michael Jackson. Colette posing for a picture standing next to Michael was the moment my mother had been waiting for.

Michael Jackson with Colette at Jacksons' thank-you party. Hayvenhurst Estate 1973.

This was the reason why my mother, who had more faith than finances, endured an uncomfortable three-day bus ride, not knowing whether we'd actually meet the Jackson 5. Why she used food stamps and welfare checks to take us to California to find the home of the hottest group, in spite of not knowing their address. Why she skipped two months' rent and risked being evicted from our small South Bronx apartment. She'd made many sacrifices for this moment.

I stood next to my mother as she was filming and heard her mumble, "Do something, it's a moving film." But Michael and Colette just stood there.

After hearing that, I decided I would take action. Like an Afro-wearing cupid, I walked up to Michael and Colette. Michael looked down at me as I approached. Colette did not know what I was going to do but suspected it would be something mischievous. I took Michael's hand and Colette's hand and placed one on top of the other. Colette was shocked and removed her hand as if I had placed it on hot coals. Michael simply smiled. Miraculously, right after that moment my mother's camera ran out of film and shut off.

"REMEMBER THE TIME"

We stayed with the Johnson family two more days before returning home. During our remaining days at their home, they asked us to share our Jackson 5 experience with them. We recalled the details of our two-day visit with the Jackson 5, the graciousness of Mrs. Jackson and the entire family, the beauty of their large estate. We told them about the humility of Michael, Marlon, Jermaine, Tito, and Jackie. How we watched them play basketball. How we met Don Cornelius, Redd Foxx, and other stars. The shyness of Michael.

Mr. and Mrs. Johnson and their daughter, Cheryl listened intently to each detail of our unbelievable experience. The Johnsons, knowing that our finances were limited, gave us food for our three-day trip back to New York. This kind family had not only provided us with food for our return trip to New York, but also allowed us to stay at their home for approximately a week after we'd found the home of the Jackson 5. On September 12, we prepared our bags for the trip home.

"Thank you so much for allowing us to stay at your home," our mother said to Mrs. Johnson.

"It was our pleasure. Feel free to visit us anytime."

Before we left, Mrs. Johnson called Martinique to inform her of our departure. Martinique and our mother exchanged kind words and pledged to keep in touch. Mr. Johnson, accompanied by his daughter, loaded our luggage into their car to take us to the bus depot in Los

Angeles. After we arrived at the depot, he assisted us in giving our bags to the bus driver for loading.

"Have a safe trip back home," Mr. Johnson said as he shook our mother's hand.

"Thanks again, for everything," she replied.

Colette and Cheryl embraced. They promised to keep up with each other by writing on a regular basis. As we boarded the bus, we looked out the window and saw the lovely family waving to us.

• • •

We returned to New York the morning of September 15, having spent almost a month away from home. L'Tanya was parked on Forty-Second Street waiting for us as we exited the bus terminal with our luggage. "How was it?" our sister asked as she helped us load our luggage into the green monster.

"Amazing!" Colette exclaimed.

We spent the entire ride to our Clason Point apartment talking about our once-in-a-lifetime experience with the Jacksons. Forty-five minutes later, we had returned to our humble apartment in the South Bronx. Though it wasn't as elegant as the Jackson estate or homes on Hayvenhurst Avenue, it also wasn't the unfortunate conditions that men, women, and children had to endure in the Los Angeles shelter were we stayed for almost a week. We were grateful for our humble apartment. However, the Jackson estate did give us a glimpse of what could be achieved through hard work and dedication.

As we approached our old screen door, we noticed the mailbox attached to our front door overflowing with letters. Our mother quickly leafed through the mail. Most of the letters contained bright red stamps that said, "PAST DUE!" A more threatening letter said, "NEW YORK CITY HOUSING AUTHORITY: EVICTION WARNING!" Colette and I read the ominous warning on the letter from the NYCHA. Noticing the concern expressions on our faces, our mother turned to us and said,

"Don't worry. I'll borrow some money from Mother Moses and get a few child support advances from your dad. We'll be OK. Besides, wasn't it worth the trip to find the Jackson 5?"

We both nodded and smiled in confirmation. After our mother unlocked four locks with four separate keys on our Fort Knox-like door, Colette climbed the stairs and headed toward her room with the cosmetics case full of *Right On!* magazines. She stood in the doorway for a moment.

Her bed was just as she left it. A large stuffed animal at the foot of the bed and at the head of the bed, four multicolored pillows, each of which contained a letter that spelled MIKE. She flopped down on her bed and gazed at all the posters of the Jackson 5 on her walls and ceiling, pictures of Michael and Jermaine on her dresser and the *Got to Be There* album cover, with a close-up image of Michael's smiling face, on her nightstand. They weren't simply fan-friendly pictures from *Right On!* magazine and other sources. The images took on a new meaning.

My mother and I came upstairs and saw Colette gazing at the many posters and pictures of the Jackson 5.

"Hey!" I said as I pointed to one of the posters, "doesn't that look like their backyard?" It was a poster of the brothers lying in a lush grassy area. "Yes!" Colette said,

"There it is!" Colette shouted. "That's the badminton court." She pointed to a poster of Michael with a racquet in his hand waiting for the birdie to approach his side of the net.

"There's the game room! Right there behind the Jackson 5! Where Janet and I took pictures and hung out!" I said. The Jackson 5 surrounded a small tree nearby, and Michael sat above them on a tree limb.

It was as if the posters on Colette's bedroom walls and ceiling had come to life. We all lay on Colette's bed and examined the posters on her walls and ceiling, looking at places where we had been on our visits. We reminisced about the wonderful experience with one of the nicest families we'd ever met. We talked about how casually dressed they were at the party. They looked a lot like many teenagers in our South Bronx neighborhood. We talked about Michael's shyness, Marlon's hospitality, Jermaine's congeniality, Jackie's athletic ability, and Tito's new family. Our mother spent a considerable amount of time applauding Mrs. Jackson's kindness. These images were no longer posters simply hanging on the walls and ceiling. Colette's room was now more of a family photo album. We'd come to consider the Jacksons members of our extended family. Their hospitality during our visit to their estate made us feel that way.

● ● ●

Later that day, Colette and I accompanied our mother as she walked almost three miles to the local Fotomat to get the pictures and movie film developed. Our mother filled out the envelope with her name and address and placed the Kodak camera film in an envelope. She prepared another envelope in which she placed the movie film. She handed the film to the "Fotomate," the person working at the booth.

She ripped off the perforated top of the envelope. "Your photographs will be ready in about two days and your film will be available in about five days." The friendly Fotomate handed our mother the tops of the perforated envelopes that served as receipts.

After leaving the Fotomat booth, Colette turned to our mother and asked, "Ma, do you think they will steal or ruin our pictures? If we don't get them back, my friends will never believe me." Colette's fears were not unwarranted. In the past, photos were returned to us whose images were distorted. Other times we'd submit twelve and twenty-four exposure film only to receive developed film containing no photo images.

"The film will be just fine, Colette," our mother said to assuage her daughter's fears. "We'll come back in two days to pick up the photographs." Privately, our mother prayed for the safety of the irreplaceable photographs and movies. After leaving the Fotomat booth, we walked to the record store on Cozy Corner to purchase the Jackson 5's latest album, *Get It Together*. The album was released on September 12, three days after we had visited the Jackson family estate.[33] When we returned to our apartment, Colette displayed the new album cover upright behind her old record player. The cover had an orange background with G-I-T in bubble-like reddish letters with the J5 logo atop the letter I. For the remainder of the day, Colette listened and sang along to "Get It Together," "Dancing Machine," "Don't Say Goodbye Again," and "It's Too Late to Change the Time."

• • •

Our journey to the Jacksons resulted in our missing our first full week of school. The missed school days were a small price to pay for an adventure of a lifetime. On her first day back to school, Colette walked across the alleyway toward the stone steps leading to the schoolyard. Colette's friends were sitting in their usual spots on the stone stairs. "Hey, Colette, we thought you were never coming back to school," Roxanne joked. "Where've you been, girl?"

"Rox, you will never guess where I was."

"Where?" asked Pat.

"Los Angeles, California!"

"Wow, is it as pretty as it looks on those TV shows? It seems like the sun always shines there," said Porscha.

"It is beautiful there, and everyday we were there was a sunny day."

"How did you get there?" Pat asked.

"By bus. It took us three days."

"What! Was it worth it?" Roxanne asked.

"Yes," Colette said. "You'll never guess who I met there."

"Who?" they all asked in unison.

"The Jackson 5!" As before, Pat looked at Colette in disbelief. "C'mon, girl. You know you're lying!"

"Sure, Colette, sure you did," Porscha said sarcastically. Just like the time she told her friends she had tickets to the Jackson 5 concert, Colette once again had to prove herself. "I'm telling you the truth. We spent a

---

33 "Get It Together," https://en.wikipedia.org/wiki/G.I.T.:_Get_It_Together, (July 6, 2013).

day at their house and then got invited back for a party. We met all the members of the Jackson 5 and other members of their family."

"I can't believe it! Did you take pictures?" Roxanne asked.

"Yes, my mother took still pictures and movie pictures. We just took them, yesterday, to the Fotomat booth. We should have the pictures in a few days."

"Well, I'll believe it when I see it," Pat retorted. Colette spent the next couple of days worrying about the film. Each day felt like a week. The photographs and film were Colette's only proof that she had met the Jacksons. Colette wasn't the only one who had to prove herself to her friends. I had a similar experience when I talked about my visit with the Jacksons.

My friends Angel, Denise, Gilbert, Eric, and Jeff were in front of our apartment playing punch ball, the neighborhood pastime. I ran out to tell them about my adventure to California. "What's up y'all?"

"Hey, Goog!" Denise and others often used the shortened version of my nickname.

"Que pasa?" Angel added.

"Man, I just came back from California! You guys will never guess who I met while I was there."

"Who, man?" Jeff asked.

"The Jackson 5 and their whole family!"

Eric, waving his hand at me in utter disbelief, said, "No way! C'mon, Googie, there is no way you met the Jackson family!"

"I did, man! I met Janet, too. Her and I hung out. We watched Disney cartoons. Their TV was humongous! Biggest TV I've ever seen. The TV was so big, Mickey was about my size!"

"C'mon, Goog. You hung out with Janet?" Gilbert asked with an expression of doubt.

"Why would he make this up?" Denise, the neighborhood all-star punch-ball player, asked the group of boys.

"Get outta the way, man. We're trying to play punch ball. We don't have time for those fairy-tale stories," Jeff said.

"I'm telling y'all the truth. We took pictures."

"OK, Goog. Show them to us," Gilbert challenged.

"We don't have them right now."

"That's just what I thought," said Jeff. Looking to the rest of the players as if to ignore me, Jeff screamed, "Play ball!"

"OK, when I get the pictures, I will show you guys. Cool?"

"Sure, Goog," Gilbert said sarcastically. "You want to play punch ball or what? We can use another man."

"Sure, I'll play third brick." I claimed the position I would play on the field. I wouldn't discuss my visit with the Jackson 5 and their family again until the photographs were developed.

Two days later, our mother took us back to the Fotomat booth to pick up our photographs of the Jacksons. Colette and I looked on with anticipation as our mother slowly opened the envelope, hoping the images would be clear. Colette released her usual scream when she saw the images.

The photographs were flawless. Each one allowed us to relive our memorable time with the Jacksons. Noticing our smiles and chatter, the Fotomate said, "Those must be some great pictures."

Our mother showed the pictures to the Fotomate, who said, "Oh, my God! Is that Michael? Is that Marlon? Is that really Jackie, Jermaine, and Tito?"

"Yes," our mother said. "We visited their estate in Encino, California."

"Now I understand why y'all were smiling so much! What a wonderful experience. How were the Jacksons? Were they friendly?"

"They were a gracious and kind family. Mrs. Jackson was kind enough to give us a tour of their home," our mother replied.

"I can't believe you actually met Michael Jackson!" the Fotomate exclaimed.

"Yes. He's very humble and amazingly shy."

"He sure doesn't act shy on stage or TV!" the female attendant exclaimed. Obviously she had also seen Michael perform. "I have to tell my daughter about these pictures and your wonderful Jackson 5 story. She is a big Jackson 5 fan. She's not going to believe me!" the young woman exclaimed.

Our mother continued, "I filmed our second visit with the Jackson 5 and their family. They invited us back to their home for a party."

"What? You got invited back to the Jackson home for a party?" the woman asked in utter disbelief. She quickly grabbed a pen and Fotomat envelope to write her telephone number on the back. "Would you mind giving me a call when you are ready to show your home movie of the Jacksons?" She handed our mother the envelope with her number. "My daughter and I would love to watch it. We live in Bronxdale. My name is Geraldine."

"Sure, Geraldine, I'll give you a call."

On our walk back to our apartment, Colette asked, "Ma, can I take the pictures to school tomorrow? I gotta show my friends!"

"No. If your friends want to see them, they can come to our apartment to look at the pictures. These pictures do not leave the apartment."

When we arrived at our apartment, Colette took the photographs of the Jackson family and added them to the sea of Jackson 5 posters and album covers. Colette prominently displayed the photographs along the top of her headboard.

The next day at school, Colette's friends asked about the pictures of her and members of the Jackson 5.

"Well, Colette, did you bring the pictures?" Pat asked cynically.

"No. They are at my apartment. After the three o'clock bell, you guys can come and check them out."

After the bell rang, Colette met her friends on the schoolyard steps. They raced to our apartment. They all rushed up to Colette's bedroom.

Noticing my mother sitting in her bedroom on the edge of her bed, each girl politely said, "Hi, Ms. Luckie."

"There they are," Colette said, proudly pointing at the pictures lined up along her headboard. All of the girls screamed.

"I can't believe it! That's Jackie!" Pat exclaimed.

"Look at Marlon," Roxanne said and then grabbed the picture holding it close to her heart.

"There's Michael, Jermaine, and Tito!" Porscha exclaimed.

"Is that Mrs. Jackson?" Lori asked.

"Yes, she was really nice," said Colette.

Colette's friends looked at the pictures in amazement.

I returned from school and heard the commotion in my sister's room. At once, I headed back to the front door and called out to my punch-ball teammates. "Hey, you guys want to see the pictures of us with the Jackson 5?"

They ran up the stairs to Colette's room, politely greeting my mother as they passed her door. My friends looked at the pictures in utter amazement.

"Wow, Goog. I guess you were telling the truth after all," my friend Gilbert said.

"I can't believe y'all met the Jackson 5," Porscha said.

"Well, believe it. Anything is possible, if you believe," our mother interjected as she stood in Colette's doorway. She consistently attempted to teach life lessons to Colette, our friends, and me.

Amazed by our pictures with members of the Jackson family, our friends asked rapid-fire questions. Colette and I answered every question.

"How big is the Jackson home?" my punch-ball teammate Denise asked.

"Were the Jackson's friendly?" asked Pat.

"Were Michael, Marlon, Jermaine, Tito, and Jackie cool?" Gilbert asked.

"Was Mrs. Jackson nice?" asked Porscha.

"Which member of the Jackson 5 did you meet first?" Jeff asked.

"Did you meet other members of the Jackson family?" asked Lori.

Colette and I then began to refer to our personal pictures with members of the Jacksons and *Right On!* posters on Colette's bedroom walls as we continued to tell about our experience. I pointed at the picture of my mother at the Jackson estate. "See where my mom is standing? That's where Janet and I walked near the pool." Pointing at one of Colette's posters, I said, "That's their game room. The Jackson 5 had all the pinball games you could ever dream of!"

Colette pointed to a poster showing the Jacksons at their Hayvenhurst estate and said, "I was actually standing right there!" Then she and her friends screamed in unison. "Colette, I can't believe you met Michael. How did he act?" asked Roxanne.

"Michael was friendly and very shy," Colette responded.

"Colette was shy, too," our mother said with a smirk on her face.

"Did you kiss him?" asked Roxanne.

Colette was silent.

"Nah, she was afraid of Michael!" I said.

"Shut up, Googie!" Colette said, embarrassed by my comment.

"But Ma kissed him," I said.

"Did you, Ms. Luckie?" Lori asked.

"Yes," our mother said and smiled.

Colette's friends screamed in unison.

"How was it to kiss him, Ms. Luckie?" asked Lori.

"Lori, his cheek was very soft. It was like kissing a chocolate-colored cloud."

The girls swooned as my mother shared her moment with Michael.

"He truly is shy," my mother continued. "It's amazing—he can perform in front of thousands, but he was shy around Colette, Googie, and me. We also have a home movie of Michael and other members of the Jacksons at their party."

"What party?" Roxanne asked. "Ms. Luckie, we'd love to watch the film."

• • •

Like wild fire, word spread throughout Clason Point, Soundview, Bronx River, Bronxdale, Sackwern, Castle Hill, and other neighboring projects that the Luckie family had met the Jackson 5. We were instantly the talk of the projects. Neighborhood boys and girls—and their parents—began to visit our apartment to see the pictures. Our acquaintances brought by their friends and family members. Then there were others who were strangers but had heard through the grapevine that we had met the Jackson family and had pictures to prove it.

One attractive African American middle-aged woman asked, "Are there movies of Michael, Marlon, Jermaine, Tito, and Jackie?"

"Yes, and many other stars as well," my mother replied.

"I will definitely be back! I'll bring my kids, too."

All day, men, women, boys, and girls knocked on our screen door and asked my mother whether she had received the film. "Not yet. Come back on Friday at eight."

• • •

On Friday, we returned to the Fotomat booth to pick up our movie reel. We approached the small booth with the pyramid-shaped gold roof to find Geraldine, the friendly Fotomate, smiling, our envelope in her hand. "Hi, Sodonia. I think this is what we've been waiting for." Apparently Geraldine was also counting the days until the film was produced. Our mother opened the envelope to find a gray reel of film. "Yep, this is it!" our mother replied. Colette, I, and many others in the neighborhood eagerly anticipated viewing my mother's filmed coverage of one of the most famous families in the world. "Let your daughter know that we are going to have a showing tonight at eight. We live at 738 Metcalf Avenue in Clason Point."

"We'll be there!" Geraldine replied. After leaving Fotomat, our mother turned to us and said, "Tell your friends we're going to show the movie tonight, outside in the front yard. They can invite friends and family if they'd like."

Colette and I told our friends, who told their parents and friends. At seven, my mother began to set up her film equipment in our small front yard. It was a beautiful summer evening. The sky was so clear you could count every twinkling star. There would be more stars that would appear on our movie screen come show time.

She had a portable screen. The projector looked like a small dark-gray metal safe and weighed about five pounds. Our mother set the projector on an old table and put a book under one of the legs to keep it steady. She removed the cover that camouflaged the projector bulb, reel arms and other switches.

The focus feature on the Super 8 projector rarely worked, and we couldn't afford to get it fixed. Instead, my mother would position the camera a certain distance from the screen to maintain a focused image. If the projector was too close to the screen, faces and images were completely distorted. Too far from the screen and the images would be too small to view. She'd have to spend several minutes to determine the proper distance from the screen to provide the clearest picture.

By seven thirty, Colette's friends had arrived for the showing of our Jackson 5 home movie. They brought blankets, spread them out on the grass, and sat near the screen. Many of my friends showed up with their parents. Some of the parents brought soda and popcorn. Geraldine arrived with her daughter.

The news of the premier showing of our home movie with the Jacksons had spread fast. Children and adults we did not know began to arrive at our apartment. "We heard you were showing a family video of your family and the Jacksons. Can we watch?"

People passing by asked my mother what she was doing.

"We are going to show a home movie of our visit with the Jackson 5 and their family."

Some responded, "No way!" Others asked, "What time?" Still others shouted, "Hold my spot!" They claimed an area in front of our apartment before running home to get lawn chairs. There were many men, women, and children that congregated in front of our apartment. Some sat on our stoop, others on the grass, while still others stood. My mother asked my brothers, Cecil and Robert, to get lawn chairs from our backyard for the elderly. Neighbors ran home for their own lawn chairs. This was turning out to be one of the biggest home movie premiers in the South Bronx.

Before the show, our mother decided to create a theatrical environment. She provided me with twelve-by-twelve-inch cardboard signs and instructed me to stand in front of the screen and display the signs to the audience. When I walked in front of the screen, the crowd quieted down. Without saying a word, I displayed a multicolored festive sign that read, A SUPER 8 SUPERSPECTACULAR! Everyone cheered. I then displayed the second sign that showed a grandfather clock: REMEMBER THE TIME. The crowd cheered again. Our mother, the consummate raconteur, gave a summary of our journey before starting our family home movie. She told the story of how we took a three-day bus ride on Greyhound across the country without having the address of the Jackson 5. How we stayed in a shelter for several days. How she rang many intercoms on Hayvenhurst to discover where the Jacksons lived. The graciousness of Mrs. Jackson to "allow a family of complete strangers, the Luckies, from the Bronx," into their lovely home.

The audience listened to the story in amazement. As the home movie began, the crowd became totally silent. Our mother instructed Colette to play the *Get It Together* album as background music while our silent home movie played. The audience looked on in amazement as the various stars crossed our small screen. When a member of the Jackson 5 graced the screen, females young and old erupted in screams. Some reached their hands toward the screen as if to touch the Jacksons.

Many in the audience began to call out names of stars they recognized. "Hey, look at Jackie and Marlon playing basketball! I can't believe they know how to play."

Roxanne, a Marlon Jackson fan, pointed at the screen and screamed as Marlon posed to take a picture with Colette. "There's Marlon! He is so cute! Was he nice, Colette? Did you kiss him? How did he smell?"

"Girl, you're so crazy!" Colette retorted without directly answering Roxanne's question.

Girls screamed as Jermaine's handsome face appeared on the screen. Colette's friend Porscha stood up. "Watch it, sucka, that's my man!" she said like Aunt Esther from *Sanford and Son*. The audience erupted in laughter.

The crowd was amazed by the size of the Jackson estate. "The Jacksons' backyard is like ten of ours put together," one neighbor quipped. Kids pointed to the Jackson's pool and slide and said, "Wow, that's bigger than the public pool in Bronxdale! And it has a slide!"

"There's the game room I was talking about, guys," I said to my friends when we saw the neon lights from pinball machines through the windows.

"They have a game room?" one teenager asked in disbelief.

"Yeah, and there's Janet, beside you," Angel said as the film showed me, with Janet and other young kids, standing on the steps in front of the game room.

"Wow, look. There's Fred Sanford," a man shouted, referring to Redd Foxx.

"He looks real cool in that outfit," a woman added.

A man quoted Fred. "I'm comin' to join you, Elizabeth!"

"Oh shut up, you fish-eyed fool," the gentleman's wife said, imitating Aunt Esther. Everyone laughed at the couple and then began to sing the theme song of *Sanford and Son*.

Suddenly, my friend Gilbert shouted, "Hey, there's Googie! And look—Janet is following him!" Other boys hooted and slapped me five. As Mrs. Jackson crossed the screen, a parent asked our mother, "How was Mrs. Jackson?"

"She is a gracious woman. She's very humble and kind."

"Is that Tito's new baby? Is that his beautiful wife in the dark hat?"

"Yes. She's very pretty, and the baby was so cute," Colette answered.

Geraldine's daughter asked, "Where's Michael?"

His handsome face and dazzling smile appeared on the screen. "Oh, there he is! He is so cute!" Michael walked along the poolside greeting party guests.

"Ms. Luckie. Can you stop the film so we can see his face?" the young girl requested. This request was a difficult one as the Super 8 projector did not have a pause button. Our mother had to start and stop the film several times before capturing his face. Finally, she was able to stop the film with a clear shot of Michael's handsome face. All the teenage girls screamed hysterically.

Colette got up from her spot on the lawn, walked up to the screen, and planted a kiss on Michael's face. "You should have done that when you were there!" our mother heckled.

"Did you kiss him?" the young girl asked Colette.

"No. But I did," my mother interjected.

The crowd cheered. My mother stopped the film briefly to share how she kissed Michael on his cheek during our first visit with the Jacksons.

A teenage boy said, "Those pants Michael is wearing are real cool," referring to the slacks with the gold-colored studs along each leg.

"Hey, what happened to Randy's leg? Why is he wearing a cast?" a little girl asked.

"Hey, look at Googie with Jermaine! Googie's Afro is just as big as Jermaine's! You guys look like hermanos," my Nuyorican friend Angel said as he pointed at the screen.

There were more oohs and ahhs at the shots of the buffet tables, waiters serving guests, and the Jacksons' cars. "That's Jermaine's car," I exclaimed as I pointed to the tomato-red Benz.

"That's my car!" one kid shouted out in the spirit of the game that Colette and I played on the bus.

My mother narrated a scene at the back of the Jackson home. "I'm telling Colette, 'It's getting dark, and you have to take a picture with Michael.' See how she is now coming from the back of the house?"

I took over. "Colette was so afraid of Michael that I had to take her to him." Everyone watched me take Colette's hand and escort her to Michael Jackson, who was sitting on the trunk of the luxurious green car.

A young girl asked, "Colette, did you kiss him or hold his hand?"

Colette was ashamed to give her answer. Instead, she placed her face in the palms of her hands in embarrassment.

I answered for her. "No, I had to put their hands together. Watch."

I approached him and Colette. I placed Colette's hand on top of Michael. Colette quickly removed hers. The film ended.

Everyone applauded and cheered. My mother began to pack her home movie equipment, but approximately twenty more people showed up to see our movie.

"We heard y'all were showing a home movie of the Jackson 5. Is it over?" a teenage girl asked.

Our mother couldn't bear to tell her and the group of people behind her that it was over, so she unfolded the lawn chairs, reset the projector screen, and started showing the movie again. Many of those who had watched the movie previously attended the second showing. Given the number of people who wanted to see our Jackson 5 home movie, our mother established show times of six, seven, and eight o'clock on weekend evenings. For several weeks, she had showings of our Jackson 5 home movie.

Many parents applauded my mother. They understood her willingness to do whatever was necessary to assist her child in living a dream.

"GET IT TOGETHER"

Following our two-day visit to their Hayvenhurst estate, we frequently watched the Jackson 5 on TV. Though they were superstars, they were more than that to my mother, Colette, and me. We considered them members of our extended family. Our mother watched them perform as proudly as if watching her own children. Colette and I cheered for them as if cheering for our siblings.

One Saturday morning in October, Colette and I were watching one of our favorite musical television programs, *Soul Train*. Many R&B singers made guest appearances including Aretha Franklin, Eddie Kendricks, Junior Walker & the Allstars, Stevie Wonder, and one of my favorites, James Brown.[34] One of our favorite parts of the show featured the Soul Train Gang dancers dancing down the Soul Train Line. Men stood on one side of the line, and women stood opposite them, forming an aisle. Couples would come down the aisle doing some of the best, and sometimes most bizarre, dance moves we'd ever seen. We'd watch these extraordinary performers not only to learn the latest dance moves, but also the latest fashion. The dancers also sported some of the latest hairdos and biggest Afros. The Soul Train Line was an urban dance version of a model runway.

Then there was the Soul Train Scramble Board, where two contestants (typically a couple) would unscramble letters to form the name

---

34, "Soul Train," http://en.wikipedia.org/wiki/Soul_Train, http://en.wikipedia.org/wiki/Don_Cornelius , (August 12, 2013).

of an African American singer, actor, actress, athlete, group, or other prominent African American. Winners of the Scramble Board were awarded Ultra Sheen and Afro Sheen hair and cosmetic products that were marketed to men, women, and children in the African American community. Rarely was any couple unable to unscramble the letters. Even I, an eight-year-old boy, was able to figure out what the unscrambled letters spelled.

On this particular Saturday, the narrator, Sid McCoy,[35] announced that the Jackson 5 would be on the show. Colette screamed, "The Jackson 5 are coming on *Soul Train!*" By this time, a relative had given our mother a small secondhand color TV. We looked forward to seeing the dazzling multicolored outfits the Jackson 5 were sure to wear. As before, our mother used her Super 8 camera to record the episode, allowing Colette to watch the episode repeatedly.

Don Cornelius stood in front of the *Soul Train* backdrop that appeared to be a front of a locomotive train with flashing red, yellow, and blue lights. In the background, "*Soul Train*" in neon lights rode on neon train tracks.

Mr. Cornelius was decked out in a powder-blue suit, a dark-blue shirt, and a tie of various shades of blue. The knot of his tie was about the size of a male fist. He also wore round-rimmed glasses and a huge Afro. With the exception of his formal TV attire, Mr. Cornelius looked no different than he did when I met him at the Jackson 5 party. Don Cornelius welcomed all viewers to the show. "We're gonna jump on off with the world-famous and most mighty Jackson 5!"[36] Colette screamed as did the female *Soul Train* dancers in the studio.

Michael wore white platform shoes, white bell-bottoms, a sparkling powder-blue vest, and a white shirt whose lapels were so long they seemed to touch the upper part of his shoulder. On Michael's right was his brother Jackie, who wore an outfit similar to Michael's, but his

35 Ibid.

36 Stephen McMillan, "The Soul Train History Book Presents: The Mighty Mighty Jackson 5!" http://soultrain.com/2012/06/18/the-soul-train-history-book-presents-the-mighty-mighty-jackson-5/, (September 27, 2013).

shirt-vest appeared to be pink. Marlon, who was at the right of Jackie, wore a sparkling dark-purple outfit with a bold white stripe coming down each pants leg, a white shirt, and white platform shoes. Tito, who was on the far right playing his guitar, wore a sparkling jacket-vest that appeared to be light purple in color. His pants were white with bold light-purple lines down the front. He also wore a white shirt with long lapels, and white platform shoes. To Michael's left was Jermaine, playing bass guitar and wearing a powder-blue suit with white accents, white platform shoes, and a sparkling white shirt with long lapels. In the background was the Jackson's youngest brother, Randy, playing the congas. Like Marlon, Randy also wore a sparkling purple outfit with white trimming and a dazzling white shirt.

"They look sharp!" I said to my mother.

"Yes, those outfits are nice. And look at those nice patent-leather shoes."

They all sported Afros. Outside of their dazzling outfits, the Jacksons looked exactly as they did when we met them. They performed a hit song from their new *Get It Together* album called "Dancin' Machine." The song started with a unique echoing trumpet call before the Jacksons started singing. The brothers sang in unison, "Dancin', dancin', dancin'…She's a dancin' machine…" Their dance moves were perfectly choreographed and executed. Their large Afros bounced with every move.

Michael led the song. His microphone did not remain on its stand long. In a James Brown-like motion, Michael spun several times, came to an abrupt stop in front of the microphone stand, and snatched the microphone. He sang the next verse of the song without missing a beat. How Michael was able to dance without getting his feet tangled in the microphone cord was nothing short of amazing.

In many of the Jackson 5 hits, there was typically a part of the song where Michael could put his dance moves on display. In our neighborhood, we referred to this particular part of the song as "the breaking part." The breaking part of this song sounded more mechanical. More robotic. Suddenly, Michael started doing a dance called the robot. He slid across the stage, bending and twisting at the waist. He stiffened his body and moved his arms and legs as if they were mechanical, while maintaining a robot-like expression on his face. As Michael danced, Colette screamed. Michael performed the robot with such perfection it was as if he became one right before our eyes. Members of the Soul Train Gang cheered. Colette and I cheered as well.

"I can't believe we actually went to their house and met them!" Colette said as she watched Michael's every move.

Colette and I sang along with the Jackson 5 as they sang the chorus. Michael improvised across the chorus while spinning like one of the tops I played with outside. The *Soul Train* dancers applauded following the Jackson 5 performance. We applauded as well.

Don Cornelius joined the Jackson 5 on stage to interview them. Every time there was a close up of Michael, Colette planted a kiss on the TV screen as if to kiss him on the cheek.

"Now that you are three thousand miles away, you can kiss him on the cheek? Why didn't you do that while you were next to him?" our mother playfully said to Colette.

"I don't know. I was so scared," Colette responded in an attempt to explain her star-struck behavior when she'd met Michael Jackson.

After Don Cornelius interviewed the members of the Jackson 5, he said that they would perform again after the commercial break. The Jackson 5 being featured during the entire one-hour show was a pleasant surprise. Typically, *Soul Train* would have two or more artists perform and include special guest stars such as Bill Russell, Jim Brown, Richard Pryor, Pam Grier, Fred "the Hammer" Williamson, and other famous athletes, comedians, actors, and actresses. Following the commercial break, featuring Ultra Sheen and Afro Sheen hair products, Don Cornelius introduced Mr. Jackson, who sported a tan leather jacket, a brown shirt with large lapels, and an Afro.

"Hey, there's Mr. Jackson!" I said, remembering him from our visit with the Jackson 5. Mr. Jackson described how the Jackson 5 got started. How he and the Jackson 5 traveled from Gary, Indiana, to Chicago during the cold winter months to perform at small shows and nightclubs[37] and would later do bigger shows at the world-famous Apollo and Regal theaters. Mr. Jackson described the hard work, endless rehearsals, and dedication that were required for the Jackson 5 to reach superstar status.

As Mr. Jackson talked, my mother said, "Wow, those boys sure look like Mrs. and Mr. Jackson. They all have that Jackson smile."

Don Cornelius then introduced a film clip of the thank-you party. "Oh my God, we were there!" Colette screamed. The film clip showed the swimming pool, buffet, dining tables and chairs, and attendants preparing for the thank-you party. The film clip looked like our own home movie.

Our phone rang. Colette picked it up. It was Roxanne.

"Girl, are you watching *Soul Train*? Their film clip looks just like the home movie your mom showed us the other night!"

"I know. This is wild! I can't believe I'm watching this!" Colette replied.

Shortly after, Colette's other teenage friends were frantically knocking at the door and yelling through the screen door, "Colette, the Jackson 5 are on *Soul Train*. The show is showing a film clip like the home movie your mom showed us. We tried to call you but your phone was busy."

"Come in. I'm on the phone with Roxanne right now!"

Colette's friends came into our apartment to watch the show with us as Colette kept Roxanne on the line. As the *Soul Train* film clip showed a table that displayed a buffet of fruit, I shouted, "Hey, there's the game room in the background!"

Then the *Soul Train* film clip showed the family members filing into the party from a back area one at a time: La Toya, Mrs. Jackson, Mr. Jackson, Michael, Tito, Jermaine, Marlon, and Randy (on crutches). The *Soul Train* film clip also showed Red Foxx and his female companion.

"I was sitting right over there," Colette said as the film clip showed Michael playing badminton with an acquaintance.

"Man, we stood right there!" I shouted as the film clip showed some of the Jackson brothers playing basketball in the driveway.

---

37 "Jackson 5 on *Soul Train*," http://www.youtube.com/watch?v=KLceDZo_UiI.

The film clip ended, and Mr. Cornelius concluded his interview of Mr. Jackson as "It's Too Late to Change the Time," a single from the *Get It Together* album played in the background. Don Cornelius reintroduced the Jackson 5.

As the Jackson 5 performed, the dancers were "pop-locking," doing splits and other moves. Many of the dancers wore Afros that bounced as they danced. Some guys also wore oversize suspenders that were more of an accessory than to keep their pants in place. Between the members of the Jackson 5 and those of the Soul Train Gang, we were watching some of the best dancers in the world.

For their final selection, the Jackson 5 sang a beautiful ballad called "Don't Say Goodbye Again." Colette sang along with her eyes closed as tears streamed down her caramel-brown cheeks. As the show ended, Colette, our mother, and I joined Don Cornelius in his typical closing statements. "And you can bet your last money, it's all gonna be a stone gas, honey! I'm Don Cornelius, and as always, in parting, we wish you love, peace and…Soul!"

● ● ●

During January 1974, Colette took one of many frequent trips to the store to collect *Right On!* magazines. Colette was filled with joy when she read that the Jackson 5 were scheduled to begin their US "G.I.T.: Get It Together" tour in February 1974.

"Ma, the Jackson 5 are touring again!" she said to our mother as she entered our apartment.

"So when are the Jackson 5 coming to New York, Colette?"

Colette pulled out her *Right On!* and ran her finger down the tour schedule.[38]

- February 22–Houston, Texas Astrodome
- April 26–Lake Tahoe, Nevada Sahara Tahoe Hotel

---

38 "Jackson 5 Concerts," http://www.jackson5abc.com/ dossiers/concerts/ (September 13, 2013).

- May 13⁻Washington, DC, RFK Stadium
- June 22⁻Los Angeles, California Forum
- June 24⁻Chicago, Illinois Mill Run Theatre
- July 15⁻Pittsburgh, Three Rivers Stadium
- July 21⁻Richmond, Virginia Coliseum

"Here we are. July 27, New York, Madison Square Garden." Colette pointed at the date in the magazine.

"This time," my mother said while looking at me, "we're all going to see the Jackson 5." Our mother felt that we had a special connection to the Jackson family. She saw our attendance at the concert as a family reunion of sorts. To purchase tickets for herself, Colette and me, our mother would spend the next several months saving as much money as possible.

A few days before the "Get It Together" concert, Colette spent hours pondering what she would wear. She put on different outfits and showed them to our mother like a model walking a runway. "What about this, Ma?" Colette asked as she came out in white hot-pant shorts and a tube top.

"All of your outfits are cute, Colette. But what you should do is wear the lavender-colored outfit you wore to the party."

"No way! Then they will see me in the exact same outfit I wore almost a year ago!" Colette assumed the members of the Jackson 5 would not only remember her but also notice her in a sea of screaming teenage girls.

"Well, Colette, I believe if you wear your lavender outfit, there's an even better chance they will see you and remember you."

Colette accepted our mother's advice. The day of the concert, our mother pressed Colette's lavender outfit. She also permed Colette's hair. Instead of the huge beach-ball-size Afro Colette regularly wore, her hair was silky smooth and flowed down to her shoulders.

We took public transportation to Madison Square Garden, arriving approximately one hour before the show. We made a brief stop at the souvenir stand. Colette purchased paraphernalia to add to the Jackson 5 merchandise and posters she had accumulated since 1970. Before leaving the stand, Colette noticed a familiar face at a neighboring souvenir stand. It was Sharon, the beautiful girl Colette had met on our bus ride from New York City to Los Angeles.

"Sharon!" shouted Colette. They ran to each other and embraced. Sharon introduced Colette and our mother to her mother.

"So this is the girl who sent you the lovely stationery with the beautiful penmanship describing how she met the Jackson 5," Sharon's mother said.

Since our visit to California, Sharon and Colette had become pen pals. Colette had written Sharon about her unforgettable experience with the Jacksons.

"Where are you sitting, Colette?" Sharon asked.

"In the orchestra section," Colette proudly said. "What about you, Sharon?"

"Girl, I'm in the green section. The seats are so high up, my nose is going to bleed."

We all laughed. Colette and Sharon embraced once more before heading to their respective sections of Madison Square Garden.

We sat approximately tenth row center, giving us an outstanding view of the entire stage. On the stage were electric pianos, drums, and other instruments. Our mother pulled out her Super 8 camera. She planned to film the entire concert and store it with other recordings of the Jacksons, including our film of the thank-you party. The concert MC was Frankie "Hollywood" Crocker, the famous New York City radio DJ from WBLS.[39] He was tall and slender and had permed black hair that came down to his shoulders.

I innocently said to my mother, "Ma, he looks like Jesus."

She smiled at my comment and refocused her attention on the stage. Frankie Crocker's voice was thunderous. Women and girls screamed hysterically with every word he spoke. He introduced the first act, a female

---

39 "Frankie Crocker," http://en.wikipedia.org/wiki/Frankie_Crocker, (March 17, 2014).

group called MDLT (Maxine, Diane, LaVerne, and Tina) Willis.[40] The group was comprised of four sisters who, like the Jackson 5, were from the Midwest and were managed by Joseph Jackson. They were dressed in white bikini-like tops with fitted bell-bottom pants that accentuated their voluptuous hourglass figures. Their outfits resembled the outfit that Colette wore to the concert and the party. The group performed their new single "What's Your Game."

Shortly thereafter, Frankie Crocker introduced a group gaining in popularity for their heavy funk and R&B style of music. The group, also from the Midwest, was called the Ohio Players. They wore colorful outfits and big Afros, and the music they played was electrifying. They played drums, guitars, trumpets, trombones, and saxophones. The lead singer, Leroy "Sugar Foot" Bonner, sported a unique Afro. The front left side of his 'fro hung so low that it draped over his left eye like a pirate's patch. He also played the most unique instrument I'd ever seen, a double-neck guitar. They performed several songs including their big hit "Skin Tight." The group left to thunderous applause from the audience.

Following a brief intermission, the lights went out. Unlike the opening acts, the Jackson 5 needed no introduction. The Garden erupted in screams by teen girls and women—I had to cover my ears. The stage lights came on and five young boys seemed to glide out onto the stage. The Jackson 5 were dressed in white outfits with black trim down the pants legs, with matching black trim across their jacket lapels, and white patent-leather shoes. Stitched on the front of their jumpsuits was "J5" in bold black letters. They all sported huge Afros, Jermaine's being the largest, that bounced with every move. A full band accompanied them, including their younger brother Randy, who played the congas.

The Jackson 5 sang a medley of songs, both old and new. They also performed their new hit "Get It Together," the title track from their recent album and the namesake of the tour. The entire audience, including Colette and me, sang along with the Jackson 5 as if we were members

---

40 "Secrets Confidential, Joe Jackson Girl Group," http://secretsconfidential.blogspot. com/2013/03/the-jackson-five-produced-girl-group-in.html, (September 16, 2013).

of the group. Colette sang these songs with tears of joy in her eyes. Our mother also sang along as she filmed the concert using her Super 8 camera. She held the camera above her head, periodically switching hands when her arm became fatigued.

Suddenly, the intro for "Dancing Machine" started—the sound of a trumpet call followed by a soul-funk-disco-driven beat. The crowd roared. The dancing started with a leg kick and the clap of their hands that accentuated the beat of the song. Michael sang the lead and danced while his brothers sang "Ooo-bop, do-do, bop" in the background. Michael then snatched the microphone off its stand and sang as he glided across the stage, periodically tossing his head back in a whiplash-like motion. He spun several times in a row, coming to a complete stop before his next lyric.

"Ma, he spins like my spinning-top!" I said.

My mother nodded in confirmation as she continued to film with her Super 8 camera.

Michael got the crowd involved by using a call-and-response technique. He would sing a rhythm and point his microphone at the crowd as a sign for us to sing the same rhythm. Whatever Michael sang, the roaring crowd sang in response. During the mechanical-sounding breaking part, Michael stepped to the forefront and started doing the robot. It was unbelievable.

The screams hit a climactic pitch as Michael danced. Colette and thousands of women went wild. Some cheered. Others, like Colette, cried tears of joy. Michael had a tremendous effect on the audience. This was the young superstar who walked through the thank-you party kindly greeting guests but avoiding attention. How he sweetly accepted my request to pose for a picture with my sister, Colette. During the performance, I reminisced about our interaction with the other members of the Jacksons during our visit. As I watched Marlon sing and dance, I remembered how congenial he was, and he remembered and welcomed us when we returned for the party.

While Jermaine sang, I thought of him driving that tomato-red Benz. His warm welcome to the Jackson Hayvenhurst estate made Colette burst into tears of joy. I thought about how he took time away from the party to take a picture with me, a little boy from the Bronx whose Afro was as big as his. I watched Tito passionately strum his guitar and remembered him walking around the party with Dee Dee, proudly introducing their first son, "TAJ", to guests.

While Jackie sang, danced, and played a tambourine, I thought of how he skillfully played basketball with his friends in the driveway, how, in spite of being in a bit of a rush, he took out the time to pose with Colette for a picture. In the percussion section, I saw Randy rhythmically beating the congas. I remembered how he hobbled about on crutches as he moved about the party.

When the show ended, the Jackson 5 walked to the front of the stage and bowed in appreciation of the thousands of fans that had come to their performance.

The lights in the arena came up. The concert was officially over. As my mother packed her Super 8 camera, she notice a familiar face just offstage behind the percussion section. It was Mrs. Jackson. She was preparing to leave following the performance of her superstar sons. "There's Mrs. Jackson!" our mother said. "Mrs. Jackson!"

Mrs. Jackson turned around and stared for a moment. She smiled and waved. My mother, Colette, and I waved in return.

Mrs. Jackson then made a gesture I'll never forget. She began to point us out to other Jackson family members. She seemed to be reminding them of who we were. They also began to wave at us. We enthusiastically waved back. That the Jacksons remembered the Luckies from the Bronx almost a year after our visit to their estate spoke volumes about their humility, character, and genuine hospitality.

A young teenage girl and her parents noticed our brief interaction with the Jacksons. "Excuse me, ma'am. Do you know the Jacksons?"

Our mother turned to the girl and her parents and said, "Well, it was the summer of 1973, a year we'll never forget…"

EPILOGUE: LIVE IN
THE IMPOSSIBLE

When my mother decided to take my sister and me to California to search for the world-famous Jackson 5, she not only demonstrated her love for her daughter, but she also demonstrated her ability to live in the impossible. It was her uncanny ability to live in the impossible that enabled us to experience the impossible.

After Colette realized that the Jackson 5 would not return to New York City for some time following the "Skywriter" concert, she experienced a considerable amount of heartache. As if experiencing the pain of her daughter's broken heart, my mother did what any loving parent would do—whatever was humanly possible to stop the pain her child was feeling. She could have chosen an easier route to assuage her daughter's emotional pain. She could have purchased more *Right On!* magazines, so Colette could collect more images and posters of Michael Jackson and the Jackson 5. She could have bought Colette J5 paraphernalia or their latest album. My mother could have also promised to purchase concert tickets for the next Jackson 5 tour through New York City or the tri-state area. Given our mother's financial constraints, even these remedies would have come with their share of challenges. Nevertheless, they would have been possible. Any of these possible low-risk means of relieving her daughter of emotional pain would have provided some comfort with relative certainty.

However, she wanted her daughter to experience the impossible. My mother would have to live with actions that provided no guarantees and were far less comfortable than the more realistic remedies to relieve her daughter's longing to see the most popular teen group of the time. She decided to take extraordinary actions to generate impossible results.

My mother's ability to live in the impossible enabled her to go beyond her comfort zone and look beyond the obvious obstacles. To find comfort during a journey filled with uncertainty. In spite of the obstacles she faced, she did not ask why or how. She asked, "Why not?"

When we live in the relative comfort, safety, and certainty of the possible, we experience what is ordinarily possible. However, when we are able to live in the impossible and endure its vagaries, discomforts, uncertainties, and risk, we are positioned to not only experience the impossible, but also to experience something beyond what we can dream or imagine.

ACKNOWLEDGMENTS

Thanks to my mother, Sodonia Luckie, who saw beyond the obstacles and impossibilities to make her daughter's dream of meeting Michael Jackson and the Jackson 5 come true. Her unshakable faith in the impossible is an inheritance left to Colette and me that will last forever. Without my mother's immovable faith in the impossible, we'd never have had the unforgettable experience of meeting the Jacksons. Without that experience, this book would not have been written. Without this book, I would not have an inspirational story to share in an effort to encourage millions around the world to believe in the impossible.

I thank Mrs. Jackson and the Jackson family, whose gracious hospitality we will never forget.

Special thanks to my lovely wife, Sherree Luckie, whose words of encouragement and support I couldn't do without. For the unconditional love of my children, Chanel Manney-Luckie, Sloan II, and Sterling William Luckie. To my father, Sloan Harris, who instilled in me lifelong principles of discipline, focus, and hard work.

Thank you to Marion Brooks, from NBC–Chicago, who did a phenomenal job of reporting the inspirational Jackson 5 story in 2009 and has provided encouragement and support ever since; to my good friends, Jay and Patricia Hewlin, Keith and Deidra Jenkins, Monica Ramsey, and Jim Reynolds, for their support and friendship; to my friends and colleagues who've encouraged me to write this inspirational story and have waited patiently for me to pen the details.

I greatly appreciate the many family members and friends who agreed to be interviewed for this book: Colette Luckie, L'Tanya Luckie, Cecil Luckie, Mary Mines, Frank Martinez, Frances Jarvis, Brian Jarvis, Gloria Harris, and Sharon Parker.

Last but not least, I thank God for allowing me to inspire many with this story and for blessing me with an extraordinary mother, who taught me "with God, nothing is impossible." My hope is that we all begin to believe and live in the impossible.

ABOUT THE AUTHOR

Sloan Luckie is forty-eight years old and originally from the Bronx, New York. He attended Music & Art High School, attained his BSBA in accounting from the University of Hartford, and an MBA in finance from the NYU Stern School of Business. He is a certified public accountant.

Sloan, founder of Body Under Construction, LLC, is also the author of the inspirational optimal health and wellness book *Body Under Construction: How to Build and Maintain Optimal Health at Any Age.*

Sloan Luckie lives in Flossmoor, Illinois, with his wife, Sherree. They have three children, Chanel, twenty-one, Sloan II, eleven, and Sterling, eight, and a granddaughter, Peyton, one.

For more information on the author, visit **sloanluckie.com**

Made in the USA
Middletown, DE
04 March 2015